SAVE THE
ANIMALS!

SAVE THE ANIMALS!

In these days of man's obsession with the destruction of our planet some people's minds have turned to thinking about the importance of the creatures that share it with us. It is only now, almost too late, that we are realising the vital contribution they make. It is up to us to mind him, to protect him, stop eating and wearing him and using things of vanity for which he pays the ultimate price. This honest and well-thought out book will show you how to help. A much needed text in a world of much needed change.

CARLA LANE, scriptwriter and co-founder of Animaline

Separate issues joined together by compassion and concern are united still further in this marvellous, comprehensive and timely book.

Whatever people think, no voice is insignificant in the battle against animal abuse and suffering, but for those who need encouragement and a few signposts, and the knowledge that they are not alone – *Save the Animals* will supply just that.

VIRGINIA MCKENNA, actress and founder of Zoo Check

Unusually fair and clear-minded. If we all follow her reasonable well-considered suggestions, we will soon see the end of cruelty to our fellow creatures.

RUE MCCLANAHAN, co-star of The Golden Girls

Contains information that will help make life healthier, happier and more generally fulfilling for my gentle, loving and snuggly catfriend, Frida. It will also mean better lives for all her relatives and mine.

ALICE WALKER, author of *The Color Purple*

An excellent, easy-to-read book that shows the power is in our hands to save animals.

JULIET GELLATLEY, The Vegetarian Society of the United Kingdom

SAVE THE ANIMALS!

101 Easy Things You Can Do

INGRID NEWKIRK

An Imprint of HarperCollinsPublishers

AN ANGUS & ROBERTSON BOOK
An imprint of HarperCollinsPublishers Ltd

First published in the United Kingdom by
Angus & Robertson (UK) in 1991
An imprint of HarperCollinsPublishers Ltd
First published in Australia by
Collins/Angus & Robertson Australia in 1991
A division of HarperCollinsPublishers
(Australia) Pty Ltd
First published in the USA by
Warner Books Inc, New York

Angus & Robertson (UK)
77–85 Fulham Palace Road, London W6 8JB
United Kingdom
Collins/Angus & Robertson Publishers Australia
Unit 4, Eden Park, 31 Waterloo Road,
North Ryde, NSW 2113, Australia
William Collins Publishers Ltd
31 View Road, Glenfield, Auckland 10,
New Zealand

A catalogue record for this book is
available from the British Library

ISBN 0 207 17072 X

Printed in Great Britain by Cox & Wyman
Typeset in Great Britain by AKM Associates (UK) Ltd, Southall, London

Printed in soybean ink on recycled paper.

ACKNOWLEDGEMENTS

Thanks for their invaluable contributions to this book go, first and foremost, to Kym Boyman, who became my special assistant only days before the book was a 'go', who learned immediately how monumental a job she had accepted and threw herself generously and more than ably to the task; to the ever-efficient Vicky Kaempf, who smoothed the wrinkles out of every working day; to the talented PETA correspondents Christine Jackson, Teresa Gibbs, Carla and Karin Bennett, and Jill Leonard; to David Cantor for finding just the right quotes; to Karen Porreca, our meticulous librarian; to Alex Pacheco, for being my friend and inspiration; and to the tremendous team of activists who make up the PETA staff and who have personally 'animal tested' everything you will find on these pages.

My thanks to Janet Hunt for her help in adapting the text for British readers.

The information in this book regarding products that are tested on animals, and societies, is accurate as of 1 February 1991.

CONTENTS

FOREWORD

A long time ago we realised that anyone who cares about the Earth – really cares – must stop eating animals. The more we read about deforestation, water pollution, and topsoil erosion, the stronger that realisation becomes. Of course, anyone who cares about *animals* must stop eating animals. Just the thought of what happens in a slaughterhouse is enough. We stopped eating meat the day we happened to look out of our window during Sunday lunch and saw our young lambs playing happily, as kittens do, in the fields. Eating bits of them suddenly made no sense. In fact, it was revolting. If you want to live a longer and healthier life, the conclusion is exactly the same, *naturally*.

Ingrid Newkirk believes this too, with all her heart. Her book is so chock full of insights into animals' lives and needs, as well as quick facts about everything from vegetarianism to making life more pleasant for your dog or cat, that you can't help but ask why this book hasn't come along sooner. The subtitle says '101 Easy Things . . .' but that's an understatement. This small book is full of tips on creative, interesting, tangible and painless ways to be a powerful advocate for almost every kind of other-than-human being. Whether you are a musician, a carpenter, a nurse, a student, a homemaker, or even a farmer, there are suggestions that are custom written for you and can be implemented right away.

So, thanks from us, from PETA, and from the animals for caring enough to make a *big* difference. Happy reading!

LINDA MCCARTNEY

INTRODUCTION

Ingrid Newkirk has written a brave and wonderful book. She has surrounded and zeroed in on virtually every field of cruelty to our fellow creatures, and, when it comes to the perpetrators, she takes no prisoners.

With it all, she has maintained her special brand of humour, one which in my capacity as president of the Fund for Animals and also of the New England Anti-Vivisection Society (NEAVS) I have come to know, both personally and professionally, is such a vital part of her. Who but Ingrid, for example, would have chosen chapter titles like 'Mind Your "Bees" and "Shrews" ', 'Deer Editor', 'Be Fish Friendly', and 'Silver Scream'.

Her quotations are ones you won't soon forget. Take Gandhi's, for one – 'I hold that, the more helpless a creature, the more entitled it is to protection by man from the cruelty of man.' Or, for another, John Bryant – 'There are three prerequisites for angling – a hook, a line, and a stinker.'

'*Never, never, never,*' she writes, 'buy a caged bird.' And she has, for rats, 'Rat Facts', i.e., 'Number of reported cases of humans bitten by rats in New York City in 1985: 311. Number reported bitten by other people: 1,519.'

And 'rat facts' aren't the only facts you'll learn here. Try lobsters:

> Lobsters are fascinating. They have a long childhood, and an awkward adolescence. They use complicated signals to explore and establish social relationships with others. Their communications are direct and sophisticated. They flirt. Their pregnancies last nine months. Some are right-handed, some are left-handed. They've even been seen walking hand-in-hand! Some can live to be more than 150 years old . . .

Many of her statements will shock you. They should. 'See meat for what it really is,' she writes, 'antibiotic- and pesticide-laden, rotting parts of a tortured animal.' 'Alligators and snakes,' she writes again, 'are usually conscious when skinned to make shoes, handbags and belts because no one can be bothered or wants to incur the extra expense of stunning them . . .' 'Young Karakul goats are boiled alive by shepherds to produce "kid" gloves because it tenderises their skin.'

Whether you can do anything about these things is up to you. Ingrid will show you how. But here too you will find simple advice every one of us can follow every day – 'Turn that television off and resolve to walk and play daily with your faithful companion animal.'

She calls this, typically, 'Quality time'. So, too, is time spent with this extraordinary book.

CLEVELAND AMORY

PREFACE

In 1980, I helped found People for the Ethical Treatment of Animals (PETA). It happened because of a young political science student named Alex Pacheco who walked into the Washington, DC, animal shelter one day and volunteered his services. As the beleaguered person in charge, I gladly put him to work.

It turned out that only a few months earlier, Alex had been aboard the Fund for Animals' ship, *Sea Shepherd*. The vessel's captain, Paul Watson, had recruited the first group of marine mammal 'warriors', Alex among them, to hunt down a pirate whaling ship called the *Sierra*. Over the years, the *Sierra* had been responsible for butchering hundreds of whales in international waters. After combing the Atlantic, Watson and the crew of the *Sea Shepherd* found the boat off the coast of Portugal. They trailed it from a distance until it berthed in Lisbon and, when its crew was safely ashore, rammed its bow. The *Sierra* went to the bottom, never to harpoon another Great Blue again.

Alex had fled Portugal, overland, to England, where he met up with activists in the already well-established movement for animal rights. He learned how to interfere with foxhunters' cruel 'sport' by mastering the hunting horn to call away hounds; marched in Trafalgar Square for the abolition of vivisection; and adopted a meatless diet of beans on toast and soy sausage rolls.

In his backpack, Alex carried copies of *Animal Liberation*, a book that had changed his way of thinking about animals. He lent it to me and, like tens of thousands of other people in the ten years that have passed since I read it, I came to realise as I turned the pages that, deep in my heart, I believed, along with Peter Singer, the book's author, that animals have a worth in and of themselves, and that they are not inferior to human beings but rather just different from us, and that they really don't exist for us nor do they belong to us. I also realised that it should not be a question simply of *how* they should be treated within the context of their usefulness, or perceived usefulness, to us, but rather whether we have a *right* to use them at all. Surely, as Henry Beston first stated and Singer reiterated: animals are 'not our underlings, they are other nations caught with ourselves in the net of life and time'.

Over the years, I had witnessed terrible cruelties. In my work as a humane officer, I had scraped dying animals from the roads and crawled under buildings and into sewer pipes to retrieve what was left of little bodies ravaged by cars, disease, and human hands. I had held burned dogs in my arms; pulled starving horses, and even pigs, out of barns; and brought many a prosecution for wilful acts of abuse. I had glimpsed behind the laboratory doors, where animal life is a cheap commodity and other-than-human beings are not uncommonly the victims of insensitivity, even sadism. Yet even I, a person who cares deeply for animals, had never considered that perhaps showing animals the little kindnesses, like a longer chain for the guard dog, a drink of water for the carriage horse, a painkiller for the guinea pig in the laboratory, or a hammerblow to the head to stun the steer at slaughter time, just wasn't enough. I hadn't realised that the greatest kindness was really to show enough respect for others to leave the animals in peace, unmolested.

I knew that while most people are appalled at the idea of cruelty to animals, few of them will ever see how a pig becomes a pork sausage, learn how raccoon mothers' chew off their own feet in leg-hold traps to return to the babies left behind in their dens, or realise that rabbits have shampoo poured directly into their open eyes in crude tests. Like me, most people had only to be shown that such things are reality for billions of individual creatures to want to *do* something to stop the suffering.

The question was, *what* could anyone do?

By forming PETA, Alex and I created an information hub. Through meetings, publications, and public events, we created the opportunity to show people exactly what animals endure in every human endeavour – from factory farming to cosmetics tests to circuses and zoos, hunting, and even that 'peaceful' pastime, fishing. Most importantly, we felt that *knowing* the problem was only a first step and that the second step, *doing something to help*, has to be made as painless as possible in this convenience-orientated, rush-rush society.

Ten years ago, making a transition to vegetarianism, finding non-leather shoes, and choosing a lipstick that hadn't been tested on animals, was hard. There were few healthfood stores, 'cruelty-free' household products and cosmetics had to be made at home or ordered by mail, and no one publicly protested about animal acts or sued their school for the right not to cut up the frog. Today, vegetarian cookbooks bend the bookstore shelves and, for those who hate to 'give up' a food, there is a soy taste-alike for almost anything, from tofu 'ice-cream' and 'cheese' to tempeh burgers and tofu frankfurters. Companies as large as Avon, Revlon and Christian Dior Parfums have stopped hurting rabbits and other animals as part of their product testing, and designers like Giorgio Armani and Bill Blass have stopped using fur. Mr Armani has even had a label sewn inside his coats that reads, 'Thank you, Giorgio, for saving our skins.'

PETA has grown enormously. We now have more than 300,000 members throughout the US, compassionate people who actively fight 'institutionalised' animal abuse, no matter how cleverly disguised it may be behind advertising jingles, or how deeply ingrained it has become in our society. These people have switched from sloppy shoppers to caring consumers. They don't sit quietly when they know animals need their voices; they speak out. They don't accept cruelty; they fight it. Thanks to them, great changes are occurring, and the world is getting to be a better place for the other 'animal nations' who share it with us.

This book can help you become one of these people. As you read it, you join a community of others who respect animals enough to make choices that affect them. Often these are simple choices, like which movie to see or which veterinarian or beauty salon to patronise. Sometimes, they're tougher ones, like what to do with your backyard or how to deal with your child's teacher's insistence that s/he dissect. You will learn how to make your vote count, how to influence magazine publishers and television producers with a few strokes of your pen. Your neighbourhood stores will begin to reflect your choices by adding items to their shelves and even subtracting unacceptable ones, thanks to you.

If you only do a few of the things suggested in this book, you should feel good about yourself. The more you do, the better you'll feel, the happier your companion animals will be, the healthier you'll become, and the more impact you'll have on the world around you. Now, how can you beat that?

AND JUST BEFORE YOU START...

When I was asked to adapt *Save the Animals!* for British readers, my first reaction was pleasure. I at once started to send off to the many excellent societies with which this country abounds, already knowing most of the facts but needing to confirm the details. It was as the replies started to trickle and then flood in that the backlash caught me. How can so many terrible things be happening to animals, mostly in the name of greed but also under such dubious pretexts as sport, entertainment, the beauty business? How can we, proud of our reputation as a nation of animal-lovers, *let* them happen? Why aren't there marches and riots and people chaining themselves to railings?

I steeled myself to continue my research, matching up facts with chapters. And gradually I felt my spirit lighten. I realised that there *are* people fighting for animals' rights, lots of them, people mostly working on shoestring budgets, sacrificing comfort and time and even their own safety to change things, to put right at least some of the wrongs.

But what can I personally do, I thought?

Which is where Ingrid's book came into its own. As I worked through it I was struck again by the fact that this isn't just another book about animals; it's a practical manual. We don't have to wait until legislation is passed, or feel helpless and angry. This book tells you, me, anyone who cares, just what each of us as individuals can do. Even the smallest changes in our lifestyles will actually help save the lives of animals.

Read it and you'll see what I mean. Try some of the suggestions (or all of them) not just for the sake of the animals but for your own sake too. There's no better way to deal with that feeling of frustration than to take action! Go to it.

JANET HUNT

1

THE UGLY SIDE OF BEAUTY

I urge you to support the companies who have chosen to reject cruelty in the production of their goods.

JOANNA LUMLEY

If you knew what L'Oréal do to animals, it would make your hair stand on end!

STEVE MCIVOR,
National Campaign Organiser, BUAV

THE PROBLEM

Companies' slick advertisements of lipsticks, furniture polish and other cosmetics and household products never include descriptions of what happens annually to the millions of rabbits, guinea pigs and other animals still maimed and killed worldwide by many major companies in crude product tests.

The most common product tests are the Draize Eye Irritancy Test and the Lethal Dose 50 (per cent) Test. The Draize test involves dripping substances, such as nail polish and dandruff shampoo, into rabbits' eyes to study reactions (often bleeding ulcerations) during a three to twenty-one day testing period. Lethal Dose tests involve force-feeding substances, such as toilet bowl cleaner, to animals to observe reactions (including convulsions, emaciation, skin eruptions, and diarrhoea) until a certain percentage, commonly 50 per cent, of the animals die.

Don't be fooled by company claims that animal tests are required or that alternatives don't exist. At present no law in Britain mandates animal testing for cosmetics and household products – the tests are designed to limit the companies' liability in case of your lawsuit! Despite animal injuries and deaths in laboratories, hair dyes, bleaches and drain cleaners may still poison and blind you if swallowed or splashed into your eyes.

THE SOLUTION

Never fear! More than 200 companies, including the Body
Shop, Honesty and L'Arome, manufacture safe, gentle, effective
products that are tested, not on animals, but through *in vitro* (test
tube) studies, with sophisticated computer models and on
human skin (cloned or attached to volunteers!). Many of them
are committed to using known-safe ingredients (there are now
more than 600), long used by humans, rather than experiment
with new chemical combinations. In addition, many high street
supermarket chains and chemists, including Tesco, Sainsbury's
and Boots, have their own brands of skincare and toiletry
products that have not been tested on animals, though these may
still contain some animal-derived ingredients.

- Look for products with the British Union for the Abolition of
  Vivisection's (BUAV) NOT TESTED ON ANIMALS logo – a
  white rabbit on a black triangle. This is your guarantee.
- Telephone or write to companies still testing on animals (e.g.
  L'Oréal and Gillette) to let them know you will not purchase
  their products until they stop maiming animals.
- Chat over the garden fence. Most people aren't aware that
  their 'cherry red' lipstick was made with the 'blood red' of
  animal suffering.
- Organise others to encourage a company to go cruelty-free:
  pass a petition out to your friends, family, neighbours and
  school; collect products manufactured by the company; and
  send them in. This action may be 'the straw that breaks the
  company's back', leading it to abandon cruel animal tests.

RESOURCES

- The British Union for the Abolition of Vivisection (BUAV)
  publishes an *Approved Product Guide* as part of their Choose
  Cruelty-Free Campaign. The guide lists over 200 companies
  producing cosmetics, toiletries and household products that
  have not been tested on animals, specifying which of the
  non-testing manufacturers still use animal-derived ingredients, and which use only vegetarian and vegan ingredients.
  Send a SAE to 16a Crane Grove, London N7 8LB, or call
  their 'Choose Cruelty-Free' hotline on (071) 700 4232.

- Or send a large SAE to the Research Animals Department, RSPCA, The Causeway, Horsham, West Sussex RH12 1HG, for their list of over seventy-five beauty product companies which do not test on animals.

2

CLEAN UP FOR THE ANIMALS

A man is truly ethical only when he obeys the compulsion to help all life which he is able to assist, and shrinks from injuring anything that lives.
ALBERT SCHWEITZER, *The Philosophy of Civilization*

THE PROBLEM

Every year some 20 million tonnes of rubbish are collected from British dustbins. Add to that the massive amount of litter deposited along streets and roads, in forests, and in the sea, and you can see why the planet is in such a mess. Rubbish not only clogs our waterways; it also strangles fishes, birds, and mammals. Every year, millions of other-than-humans are maimed and killed by our carelessness. Sometimes they push their faces into discarded food containers to lick them clean and get their heads stuck inside. Sometimes they swallow pieces of indigestible plastic in the ocean that look to them like jellyfish. Our rubbish can be injurious, even lethal.

Chew on This

- The average Briton throws away about ten times his or her own body weight in household refuse every year. More than half of this is potentially recyclable; less than 5 per cent is actually recycled.

- Items we get through in a year include around 6 billion bottles and jars, amounting to over 1.5 million tonnes of glass. And if the drink cans we disposed of in a year were placed end to end they would reach the moon!
- Of the 45 kg of plastic each Briton uses in a year, some 15 kg consists of packaging that is thrown out immediately after a product is opened.
- Plastic six-pack rings take 450 years to degrade. Birds who dive into the water to catch fishes sometimes dive into and get strangled by these rings.
- Plastic waste dumped into the sea traps fishes, mammals, turtles, and birds in knotted tangles, causing death by starvation, drowning, strangulation, or ingestion. Some experts estimate that plastic waste alone kills more than 100,000 sea mammals and 2 million seabirds each year.
- In July 1985, a dying one-year-old sperm whale was washed ashore with a mylar (silver metallic) balloon lodged in his stomach.
- In September 1987, a half-ton leatherback turtle, disabled by a latex balloon and a 3-foot ribbon blocking his pyloric valve, received a 3-foot gash from a propellor he was unable to dodge.
- The US Office of Technology Assessment reports that the massive amount of plastic pollution produced each year poses a greater threat to marine mammals and birds than pesticides, oil spills, and contaminated run-off from the land.
- There are over fifty types of plastic in use, a few of which are now biodegradable (though the process is extremely slow), but most of which cannot be or are not recycled.

THE SOLUTION

Always, the best advice is to consume less (to 'live simply so that others may simply live'). But if we remain loyal to a consumer-oriented lifestyle, we should at least carefully dispose of everything we use and pick up after others who are not so careful. Here are a few pointers.

- Recognise that your rubbish can be a trap – a potentially lethal picnic for animals in your neighbourhood. Take the following precautions:

○ Avoid buying unnecessary plastic products. Buy juice in cardboard cartons, use wax paper instead of clingfilm, and so on.

○ Whenever possible, recycle paper, aluminium, plastic, and glass. Contact the environmental department of your local council for details of their recycling facilities; most of them now have at least a few bottle and wastepaper collection points. (If not, suggest it is time they did!) Friends of the Earth arrange paper collections in many areas – call them.

○ Tell grocery store managers that you prefer to buy products packaged in a non-polluting, environmentally friendly way. Complain to the grocer if the produce department insists on wrapping items such as cucumbers and tomatoes in clingfilm instead of selling them loose.

○ Remove any tempting morsals by rinsing out jars and other containers in which animals' heads can get caught. Screw lids back on to empty jars before disposing of them, and put sharp tops and tabs inside empty tin cans so they cannot cut tongues and throats.

○ Crush the open end of cans as flat as possible to protect other-than-humans who might otherwise get cut or caught. In the USA the National Zoo drew protests when it used an elephant named Nancy to crush cans during Washington, DC's Earth Day 1990 celebrations. Use instead a wall-mounted crusher such as the one you can buy from G. & C. Home and Leisure Supplies Ltd, Cobham Road, Pershore, Worcestershire WR10 2DL (price £12.95 incl. p&p; also on sale through various 'green' catalogues). Unfortunately it only works with softer aluminium such as Coke cans; tins in which foods are sold are usually too thick for this crusher. Make these less enticing by cleaning them thoroughly.

○ Tear open one side of tough plastic and cardboard containers so that squirrels and other small animals cannot get caught in them. Hedgehogs have died, unable to back out of inverted-pyramid yoghurt pots.

○ Snip apart plastic six-pack rings, including the inner diamond. The rings are frequently found around the necks of wildlife. In a celebrated case in Maryland, USA, Mary Beth Sweetland rescued a duck who, for months, had been ensnared in a plastic six-pack holder and was wasting away. Winning the duck's confidence took time. Mary Beth eventually lured him out of the water with cracked corn and, with a garden stake she had hidden up her sleeve, gently speared the plastic rings to the ground. With a friend's help, she snipped the plastic (over which the duck's bill had begun to grow) and released the duck back to the lake.

O Always put your rubbish inside a dustbin and cover it with a heavy lid. This keeps inquisitive animals from getting at it, and also prevents them from being trapped inside. If the bin is being tipped over, either secure it to the wall with a hook and chain, or – better still – keep it in the garage or a shed until rubbish collection day.

O Never dispose of razors and other dangerous items by dropping them loose into your other garbage. Tuck them somewhere safe such as inside empty, rinsed-out and sealed cartons.

O Take care to clean up antifreeze spills carefully (and rinse out the rags you use to do so); it is toxic, and animals are attracted to its sweet taste. Do not wash antifreeze down drains.

O When shopping, take along your own string, straw or canvas bag – these are now widely available in many styles and colours. Strong jute bags with the Traidcraft logo are available from Traidcraft, Kingsway, Gateshead NE11 0NE. The Vegetarian Society (Parkdale, Dunham Road, Altrincham, Cheshire WA14 4QG) does an attractive white cotton bag. If you must use a shrinkwrap in the kitchen, avoid clingfilm and buy instead those labelled 'plasticiser free' or 'non-PVC' which are better for the environment and you (though just as harmful to animals, so take care how you dispose of them).

• Join, create, or consider yourself the sole member of a beach brigade or park patrol:

O Pick up string, fishing line, and all plastic litter (bags, bottles, six-pack rings, pots and so on) on the beach, near streams and woods. Birds, squirrels, foxes and badgers can get tangled in or swallow such items, and the results can be fatal.

○ . . . And, please, never launch helium-filled balloons. Also, protest against any balloon launches of which you might hear. Should the balloons land in water they can be mistaken for food and cause sea dwellers to choke and suffocate.

RESOURCES

- Friends of the Earth (FOE), 26—28 Underwood Street, London N1 7JQ – for everything you need to know about recycling.
- Greenpeace, Greenpeace House, Canonbury Villas, London N1 2PN – working to clean up the seas around our coast and so make them safe for the fish and mammals to whom they are home.

3

HOW SAD IS THAT DOGGIE IN THE WINDOW?

Whatever salespeople or sentimental books may state,
wild animals do not make good pets. Captivity, no matter
how 'kind', is always cruel.
JOAN WARD-HARRIS, *Creature Comforts.*

We cannot glimpse the essential life of a caged animal,
only the shadow of [her] former beauty.
JULIA ALLEN FIELD,
'Reflections on the Death of an Elephant',
Defenders, 42, Spring 1967

THE PROBLEM

Raised without affection and stressed by shipping, animals
found in pet shops can suffer both physical and emotional
problems that cause heartbreak, headaches, and behavioural
problems for them and their human companions as they grow.
Humane officers can recount stories of 'pet' shop rejects and
sick animals being drowned in the back room, left to die, or
shipped while ill or injured to cut costs.

Puppies in Peril

While our sanctuaries are bursting at the seams with unwanted
animals looking for good homes, 'pet' shops encourage the
irresponsible and negligent proliferation of dogs and cats. Most
of the puppies they sell will have come from the notorious
puppy farms that can now be found throughout the country
(though the highest concentration is in West Wales where there
are 400 licensed breeders and over 1,200 unlicensed). At least
160,000 puppies are sold through dealers each year, the majority
of them born and raised in appalling conditions. Though these
are from pedigree stock – popular with the breeders are
yorkies, King Charles spaniels, boxers and golden retrievers –

they are often inbred. Cramped living conditions and the stress of lengthy transportation may mean that they are diseased and even dying before they leave the shop.

- Very young puppies are transported vast distances to shops in major cities. Some are exported, via Heathrow, to Southern Asian countries where animal welfare has a low priority, and those who survive the journey may well end up being used in experiments.
- The breeding females remain locked in small pens throughout their lives, producing twice yearly litters. When their bodies give out and they can no longer produce litters, they may be drowned, shot, hanged or simply dumped.
- Because of a loophole in the law, unlicensed breeding goes on unchecked without control or inspection. No one, including the RSPCA or local authorities, has power of entry. Prosecutions rely on proof of sale of puppies which is impossible to obtain once they enter the dealer network.

Exotic Exploitation

- Tortoises, so popular with children, are not in fact native to this country, and every year hundreds die during or shortly after hibernation, usually because they take in too little food during the summer and therefore have insufficient reserves to keep them going. In the wild they can live to be 150 years old.
- The Teenage Mutant Hero Turtles craze has meant that tiny and vulnerable terrapins are being imported from the USA in their thousands, many dying en route. Sold for as little as 50p each, they are a novelty almost anyone can afford. If they are lucky enough to survive and grow bigger, many of them will be discarded into canals and rivers where they face more hazards. (They also upset the ecological balance by eating baby frogs and other species.)
- Caged birds have always been popular with the British. Some of these will have been bred specially for sale in this country, but many – including parrots, parakeets and lovebirds – will have been captured in the wild. Senegal is the world's largest wild bird exporting country, trappers

catching specific birds as required by the exporters. In the case of parrots, decoy parrots have their wing feathers hacked off with a machete, then are pegged to the ground. When other birds come a net is dropped over them. Figures for mortality show that 50 per cent die from capture to export. Still we import some 30,000 each year.

Imported birds must be inspected and then quarantined for thirty-five days. Thousands of them are dead on arrival. Their deaths during the journey are caused by inadequate perches and crating, temperature extremes, capture and transport shock, overcrowding, inadequate care and ventilation, disease, suffocation, unsanitary conditions and lack of food and/or water. These stresses cause birds to peck at themselves and each other, resulting in severe injuries, including blindness.

The 'lucky' survivors will spend the rest of their lives, probably alone, chained to a perch or in a cage.

- Other beings becoming popular as 'pets' include chipmunks, monkeys of various kinds, snakes, polecats, scorpions and giant spiders. In theory any animal (even endangered species) can be imported into Britain providing one has a licence. When you buy an exotic animal (any animal not native to this country) from a dealer or 'pet' shop, you may be unwittingly contributing to a cruel and gruesome trade. Most of these terrified animals don't make it alive to Britain – it has been estimated that up to ten die for every one who makes it. Survivors are susceptible to premature death from stress, malnutrition, dehydration, improper handling, illness, or general malaise. All must then go through six months' quarantine before being allowed to go to their permanent 'homes' (most purchasers are unable or unwilling to create a habitat that even remotely resembles that of exotics in their natural homes).

THE SOLUTION

- Resist buying 'that doggie in the window' – the 'pet' shop will just replace him using the profit you bring to their business. If you want to share your home with a dog or cat, visit your local dog home or sanctuary. (And reduce the 1,000 dogs destroyed every day down to 999!) And if you really must have a pedigree dog, don't forget that they turn up in sanctuaries and dogs' homes too. Anyone who has the urge to possess animals who ordinarily live wild and free in their native lands should please think again. Living beings aren't toys or decorations, and wild animals should remain unfettered.

- Never buy animals as gifts, and tell others who may be in the market for a companion animal that there are many wonderful dogs and cats waiting at their local animal sanctuary. Leaflet outside your local 'pet' shop during peak shopping times to educate potential buyers.

- Ask your local council members to pass a law banning the sale and keeping of exotic wildlife except for rehabilitation purposes – at the moment there is nothing to stop people having exotic animals in their home or garden, providing they can convince officials that the animals cannot escape! Fight permit applications for new 'pet' shops unless they limit sales to supplies only.

RESOURCE

- Joyce Stranger, popular writer and animal protectionist, has put together a sympathetic 44-page booklet called *'I'm nobody's dog. Can I be yours?'* to help anyone re-homing a dog. Available from Glanlly, Dwyran, Anglesey, Gwynedd, Wales LL61 6YU; price £1.50 plus 50p p&p.

4

GIVE ANIMALS A VOICE

I am the voice of the voiceless;
   Through me the dumb shall speak,
Till the deaf world's ear be made to hear
   The wrongs of the wordless weak . . .

And I am my brother's keeper,
   And I will fight his fight;
And speak the word for beast and bird
   Till the world shall set things right.
                    ELLA WHEELER WILCOX (1850—1919)

Unseen they suffer
Unheard they cry . . .

                                   ANON.

THE PROBLEM

Although other species have their own languages, we have yet
to figure them out. Dolphins 'click' up to 700 times a second,
reaching frequencies twelve times higher than those audible to
humans. Elephants communicate subsonically at frequencies
too low for us to hear, rats at frequencies too high. Crows in the
south of France have dialects that puzzle (and are probably the
brunt of jokes for) crows in the northern wine country.
Chimpanzees have learned to use sign language: Washoe, a
twenty-five-year-old chimpanzee considered 'family' by
primatologist Roger Fouts, knows hundreds of signs and,
unaided, has taught her adopted son, Loulis, more than seventy
of them. Chimpanzees do not have vocal chord configurations
that would permit them to make the same sounds humans make.
Most oppressed groups of human beings can speak for themselves; but until we learn to understand other-than-human
languages, we must 'speak for the animals'.

THE SOLUTION

- Speak out! Within earshot of the shopper ahead of you in the checkout line, converse with a friend about that television documentary you saw on slaughterhouses. Have polite conversations, even with strangers, about the cruelty of fur and meat production – saying you just read a disturbing article is a good starter – particularly on public transport, in dentists' and doctors' waiting rooms, or anywhere there's an audience. Also, help meat consumers by telling them what the government prefers to keep quiet: that meat can help cause heart attacks, cancer and other fatal diseases.

- Be informed. Keeping up with what's happening in the world of animal rights means that you'll be able to speak with confidence, putting your case clearly and persuasively. Read, listen, watch relevant programmes on TV. Ring Animaline on 0898 444058 for a choice of three tapes giving general information, news of specific events, and a hotline number for urgent issues, together covering every aspect of animal-related issues – continually updated.

- If you have a group, you might be able to put out a Community Service Announcement (CSA) on local radio or TV. The requirements and lengths of these will vary from area to area, as will the cost (some are free; other regional companies require you to pay an administrative cost). You are not allowed to ask for funds via a CSA, but can request volunteers (for such things as protecting badger setts, for example, or helping in a sanctuary). You can also inform the public of a service you are offering. If the idea appeals, contact your local regional TV or radio company to see if they do offer such a scheme, and if so, for details.

- Most local and some national radio programmes are only too happy to have you call in and air your views. Don't let them down. Whether the topic is food, health, beauty, or even sex, get on the phone with an animal issue tie-in!

- Arrange a series of talks and/or debates at a local school or college, church or community centre. Contact your local branch of the Women's Institute (check in the telephone directory under Businesses). To line up speakers find out who in your community is most actively working with homeless

animals, arranging demonstrations, and promoting vegetarianism. Once you have done your homework and practised
in front of a mirror and friends, you may want to deliver your
own talks.

● Order (or have printed) leaflets to distribute. Define your
audience, and make sure your leaflet answers the questions
what, where, when, why, and who. It must tell people
specifically what they can do to help. Include a phone
number as a point of contact. Keep it concise, factual, and
readable.

● Ask local schools and universities to include an animal rights
class in the curriculum. This could, for example, include such
issues as speciesism, the nature of interests and rights, and the
use of animals for food and in experiments.

● Leave an animal rights message on your answering machine.
Messages activists have used include:

  ○ 'More than 600 million animals are slaughtered for food
  each year in Britain.'

  ○ 'Incidents of water pollution have almost trebled in the
  last ten years, the main cause being factory farming.'

  ○ 'There are 55 square feet of rainforest in a quarter-
  pound hamburger.'

  ○ 'The best thing you can do for the environment and
  yourself today is to stop eating animals.'

  ○ 'I can't come to the phone – I'm shopping for cruelty-
  free products. I would be happy to send you a list of
  companies that don't test on animals if you leave your
  name and address after the tone.'

  ○ 'Do you know where your companion animals are?
  Don't let them roam unsupervised – they may be injured
  or even stolen. And when you hang up, go and give them a
  hug.'

● Let an animal rights button speak for you. Try: MEAT IS
MURDER; IMPRISONED WITHOUT TRIAL; I WON'T
EAT YOU IF YOU DON'T EAT ME; HERE TODAY, GONE
TOMORROW; FERALS NEEDS FRIENDS; VEGANS GO
ALL THE WAY; BRIGHT EYES BURNING LIKE FIRE;
STUFF TAXIDERMISTS; RATS HAVE RIGHTS; STOP
THE MONKEY BUSINESS; PUT CALVES FIRST (all

available from Animus). Or make your own, e.g. SHAMELESS AGITATOR.

- Little cards can say a few dozen appropriate words, too. If you belong to a local animal rights group, have some made up professionally. For that close encounter with the woman in dead minks in the lift, or the man in the beaver-collar flight jacket, try: EXCUSE ME FOR APPROACHING YOU, BUT WE WOULD LIKE YOU TO MEET THE PREVIOUS OWNER OF YOUR COAT; or HERE'S WHAT YOUR FURRIER NEVER TOLD YOU. You can also buy plain white cards and carefully write or type your messages. Always be polite – the most usual response to aggression is aggression.
- Most societies now sell T-shirts and sweatshirts, hats, car stickers and other items carrying appropriate slogans. Some you might like to consider include ANIMALS ARE MY FRIENDS (T-shirt from the Humane Research Trust); SAVE THE DOLPHINS (sweatshirt from the Whale and Dolphin Conservation Society); GET WISE! ANIMALS HAVE RIGHTS (owl mug from Animal Aid); DOGS DIE IN HOT CARS (RSPCA car sticker); and Greenpeace's green umbrella.
- When sending postcards, make sure you don't waste the opportunity to pass on your message. The Mobile Animal Shop has a variety that include a series of black-and-white animal photos by Linda McCartney, Stan Eales's delightful cartoons, and BORED, LONELY AND A LONG WAY FROM HOME (goldfish).

RESOURCES
- Animus, 34 Marshall Street, London W1V 1LL.
- Humane Research Trust, Brook House, 29 Bramhall Lane South, Bramhall, Cheshire SK7 2DN.
- Whale and Dolphin Conservation Society, 19a James Street West, Bath BA1 2BT.
- Animal Aid, 7 Castle Street, Tonbridge, Kent TN9 1BH.
- RSPCA, The Causeway, Horsham, West Sussex RH12 1HG.
- Greenpeace, Greenpeace House, Canonbury Villas, London N1 2PN.
- Mobile Animal Shop, P.O. Box 10, Ryde, Isle of Wight PO33 1JX.

5

JOIN A COALITION OF PROFESSIONALS

> Responsibility is a great thing. To shoulder responsibility, not to shirk it. If we learned early in life not to avoid responsibility, the world would be brighter.
> ALBERT SCHWEITZER

THE PROBLEM

Everyone has a right to be heard on moral issues – including those that involve use of the tax money we all pay annually – yet lay people are often pompously dismissed by the professional organisations whose behaviour and opinions they are trying to change. 'We'll police ourselves,' say the psychologists. 'No outside intervention,' cry the veterinarians. Well, change can be effected internally; and animal rights activists within the professions are getting together to set about doing just that.

In the USA such groups are already notching up successes. For example, more than 20,000 physicians signed a petition condemning US Surgical Corporation for using dogs when training salespeople to use its surgical staplers (over, 1,000 dogs a year are killed after the stapling demonstrations); and American nurses united to change the age-old practice of teaching student RN's intubation by pushing a tube down kittens' throats instead of using a model. The Animal Legal Defense Fund (whose poster says WE MAY BE THE ONLY LAWYERS ON EARTH WHOSE CLIENTS ARE ALL INNOCENT!) helped to halt a Californian archery bear hunt.

To date there are only a few such groups in Britain, all of which would welcome support from their colleagues. If you are a professional, do consider joining a relevant group. Encourage others to join too. If no group exists, maybe now is the time to set one up?

RESOURCES
- Doctors in Britain Against Animal Experiments (DBAE), P.O. Box 302, London N8 9HD.
- Nurses Anti-Vivisection Movement, Hillcrest Cottages, 2 Hillcrest, Uppertown, Bonsall, Derbyshire DE4 2AW.
- Teachers for Animal Rights, 29 Lynwood Road, London SW17 8SB.
- Writers Against Experiments on Animals, Wessington Court, Woolhope, Hereford HR1 4QN.

6

TEAM UP

I get by with a little help from my friends.

THE BEATLES

THE PROBLEM
Working by yourself to change the world can be a lonely prospect; and the power of a group demonstrates that, in addition to the power of the individual, the whole is (frequently) greater than the sum of its parts. Becoming part of a team, having a support system to lean on in times of frustration, pooling information and sharing ideas with others, or just pairing up, can make your life brighter and lighten your load.

THE SOLUTION
- Link up with other people who share your concern for animals by advertising to find them: put notices on local bulletin boards, in wholefood stores, launderettes, supermarkets, community centres, libraries and bookstores (e.g. 'Person interested in animal protection issues seeks others to form a group – call Pam on 123 4567'; or 'Come and join

like-minded people who want to work for the animals and the Earth – call 123 4567'). Local radio announcers will often help if you ask them nicely; listen first so that you can judge who is most likely to be sympathetic to your cause.

- Talk to other people with dogs in the park. You know for a start that they care about animals. The same with people whose cats are always sitting by the gate and with whom you've probably already struck up an acquaintance!
- Organise a regular letter-writing/sign-making work party. When new animal legislation is pending, or a circus is visiting your town, or the whole country is preparing to celebrate World Vegetarian Day, spend a few hours with other like-minded people doing work and snacking on vegan foods. You might also like to show an animal rights film. There are many now available for hire covering various aspects of animal abuse (and advice on how to stop it!), including some specially made for young viewers.
- Advertise a monthly vegan picnic or party. If attendance is slim at first, it always picks up as word-of-mouths-receiving-great-food spreads. Before the meal, provide guests with recipe cards and nutritional facts, and get people working together on a project, like brainstorming or planning a protest rally.
- Host a cruelty-free cosmetics evening, the 1990s counterpart to Tupperware parties! Invite friends, co-workers, relatives and neighbours to sample cruelty-free perfumes and cosmetics. Though at the moment there is no one company selling door to door via representatives, there are a number of direct mail companies. Contact them with a view to possibly obtaining free or low-cost samples, explaining what you are doing. Gather together a selection of these; offer to take and send off orders for anyone who is interested. (Avon, the original company selling cosmetics door to door, has now stopped testing on animals, but beware of animal ingredients.)
- Get permission to place a permanent bulletin board (e.g., ANIMAL WORLD) in a local store or at your post office. Provide space for lost-and-found animals or those who are looking for homes (photos are a plus), animal rights information, local news about animal happenings, and group newsletters.

- Start a 'phone-tree' – a calling system designed to reach a lot of people with very little effort on any one person's part. It works this way: when you need to reach a large number of people, you call three people who each call three others, who in turn each call three more people, and so on. Keep the tree updated and be sure to toss out 'dead wood' – people who promise to make their calls but don't. Phone trees can help ensure everyone knows about meetings and demonstrations, and can mobilise activity when something comes up unexpectedly.

- If you have a computer, hook up with others on a computer network. GreenNet is a computerised communcations and information exchange service specifically for environmental, peace and human rights movements. It is part of the Association for Progressive Communications (APC) and has sister networks in the USA (PeaceNet and EcoNet), The Web in Canada, Alternex in Brazil, Nicarao in Nicaragua, Pegasus in Australia and FredsNatet (PeaceNet) in Sweden. Over 5,000 subscribers (representing about 1,000 organisations including Greenpeace, the Green Party and Friends of the Earth) use one of the APC nodes on a daily basis to exchange information around the world.

  GreenNet provides two basic services: electronic bulletin board systems ('conferences') and electronic mail. Via these it can keep you up to date with subjects as varied as wildlife, farming and animal rights, the fight to save the Antarctic, and other topical issues. To access the network you can use virtually any computer or computer terminal with a modem, and as the service costs only a fraction of the usual commercial price, it is particularly suitable for voluntary groups and even individuals. And though the network is designed to be easy to use even for those who know little about computers, there are regular training sessions in London – and always help and support at the end of a telephone. For more information contact: GreenNet, 25 Downham Road, London N1 5AA; tel. (071) 923 2624.

RESOURCES

For list of films and visual aids contact:

- Animal Aid, 7 Castle Street, Tonbridge, Kent TN9 1BH; tel. (0732) 364546.
- British Union for the Abolition of Vivisection (BUAV), 16a Crane Grove, Islington, London N7 8LB; tel. (071) 700 4888 (includes *Breaking Barriers* made by People for the Ethical Treatment of Animals (PETA), USA, showing life inside a US primate laboratory).
- Compassion in World Farming, 20 Lavant Street, Petersfield, Hampshire GU32 3EW; tel. (0730) 64208, 68863.
- Vegetarian Society (UK) Ltd., Parkdale, Dunham Road, Altrincham, Cheshire WA14 4QG; tel. (061) 928 0793. *Food Without Fear* is an especially powerful and thought-provoking 20-minute video (price £12.50 – or £9.99 to schools – plus 70p p&p).

7

EDUCATE TO LIBERATE

No army can withstand the strength of an idea whose time has come.

VICTOR HUGO

How many a man has dated a new era in his life from reading a book!

HENRY DAVID THOREAU

THE PROBLEM

When your neighbour asks 'What's wrong with bull-fighting?', 'How do you get your protein?', 'Is it true greyhounds from the track go to research?', 'Do fishes feel pain?', 'Is tobacco tested on animals?', or 'Is the leg-hold trap illegal in Europe?' do you know the answers? Or do you at least know where to direct them to find the answers?

THE SOLUTION

Though bookshelves – in both shops and libraries – are bulging with books on wildlife, there are comparatively few books covering animal rights issues. It is up to you to make sure that those that *are* published get read by as many people as possible.

- Pass on the titles and authors' names of compelling books about animal rights. Lend interested enquirers used copies, or suggest they buy their own – many of the books that set out to put the case for animal rights are in paperback, and therefore not expensive. And although you may well be able to answer specific queries, getting someone to spend time with a book will help them become more fully informed, and may convince them that they too should get active.
- Use your local library. Check through their lists and put in a reservation card for any books you know to be worth reading that they don't have (in theory they should be able to get any book, even those that are out of print). Read reviews of new books and make sure these too are added to their shelves. When buying books, public libraries aim to please everyone, but their budgets are limited. Let them know there are readers who are more concerned about what is happening to animals (and what they can do about it) than about reading the latest historical romance! Most libraries have display facilities in the entrance hallway; arrange with them that you will set up a display on animal rights, preferably having someone to staff it much of the time (who can hand out leaflets, answer questions). Point out that there will be an increased demand for relevant reading so they should stock up before the display is in place.

Here's our recommended reading list (look out too for the many new books that are now being published):

Must-Read
- *Animal Liberation*, Peter Singer (New York Review, New York). Written in 1975, reissued in 1990, and considered to be the classic animal rights primer.
- *In Defense of Animals*, edited by Peter Singer (Harper and

Row, New York, 1985). Excellent essays on factory farming, zoos, and other animal rights issues. Includes a chapter by PETA chairperson Alex Pacheco, who recounts his experiences working in the laboratory where he discovered the famous Silver Spring monkeys.

- *The Cruel Deception*, Dr Robert Sharpe (Thorsons 1988). Scientific exposé of how little we stand to gain from the use of animals in medical research, and an historical overview of how human health has improved through sanitation, fresh water and attention to social issues.

- *Chicken and Egg*, Clare Duce (Green Print 1989). Behind the scenes at the chicken battery farm. Founders of Chickens' Lib open the cage of chicken exploitation and shame the Ministry of Agriculture.

- *Assault and Battery*, Mark Gold (Pluto Press 1983). Shocking and comprehensive, Mark Gold shows how 'factory farming' and intensive animal agriculture are killing the countryside, the animals and ourselves.

- *Beyond the Bars*, edited by Virgina McKenna, Bill Travers and Jonathan Wray (Thorsons 1987). The authors explore the keeping of non-indigenous animals in captivity, and present a powerful case for allowing wild animals to remain in the wild.

- *Animal Revolution*, Richard D. Ryder (Basil Blackwell 1989). History of the humane movement, and how our society is evolving to a more compassionate world.

- *Animal Experimentation*, edited by Gill Langley (Macmillan 1989). A collection of easy-to-read scientific articles concerning how animals are used and misused in laboratories.

- *Living Without Cruelty*, Mark Gold (Green Print 1988). A practical guide on how to find cruelty-free products and go vegetarian (includes recipes).

- *Voiceless Victims*, Rebecca Hall (Wildwood House 1984). A comprehensive and convincing plea for those who cannot speak for themselves.

General Animal Rights
- *The Case for Animal Rights*, Dr Tom Regan (Routledge and Kegan Paul 1988). A philosophical discussion of animal rights.

- *Fettered Kingdoms*, John Bryant (available from the Vegan Society, 7 Battle Road, St Leonards-on-Sea, East Sussex TN37 7AA). A short, moving description of our relationship to other-than-human beings, based on the common premise that such animals are slaves.
- *Animals' Rights – Considered in Relation to Social Progress*, Henry Salt (Centaur Press, reprinted 1980). First published in 1892, Salt's book provides insight into our attitudes towards animals.
- *Animals' Rights – A Symposium*, edited by David Patterson and Richard Ryder (Centaur Press 1979). An anthology comprised of the seminal papers delivered at the first animal rights conference organised by the RSPCA and held at Cambridge University in 1977.
- *Animal Rights and Human Obligations*, Peter Singer and Tom Regan (Prentice-Hall, Englewood Cliffs, NJ, 1989, revised edition). From the commonsensical to the fantastic, animal rights essays and stories by movement philosophers and campaigners.
- *The Status of Animals*, edited by David Patterson and Mary Palmer (CAB International 1989). Brings together a wide range of experts from a large number of perspectives to consider the status of other-than-human beings in relation to many human activities.
- *Men and Beasts*, Maureen Duffy (Paladin 1984). An animal rights handbook discussing various issues. Includes a chronology of Animal Liberation Front (ALF) activities.
- *The Extended Circle*, edited by Jon Wynne-Tyson (Centaur Press 1985). The definitive collection of humane thoughts and great quotes from Aurelius to Zola.
- *Animals and Why They Matter*, Mary Midgley (Pelican 1983). A philosophical discussion.

Vivisection/ Animal Experimentation

- *Slaughter of the Innocent*, Hans Ruesch (Civitas, Swain, New York 1983). A description of the vivisection industry with graphic examples of the human health hazards of animal tests.
- *Victims of Science*, Richard Ryder (1983, available from the

National Anti-Vivisection Society, 261 Goldhawk Road, London W12 9PE).

Vegetarianism/Vegan/Factory Farming

- *Why You Don't Need Meat*, Peter Cox (Thorsons 1986). A simple guide to a healthy non-animal diet and explanation of why animal foods are dangerous to your health.
- *The Vegan Cookbook*, Alan Wakeman and Gordon Baskerville (available from the Vegan Society, 7 Battle Road, St Leonards-on-Sea, East Sussex TN37 7AA). Two hundred varied recipes ranging from the quick and simple to the 'slower or dearer or more complicated'.
- *Vegan Nutrition*, Gill Langley (available from the Vegan Society, see above). An excellent sourcebook and guide.
- *Cooking with Sea Vegetables*, Peter and Montse Bradford (available from the Vegan Society, see above). Ways to cook and enjoy the harvest of the oceans.
- *The Power of Your Plate*, Neal Barnard, MD (Airlift Distributors 1990). A collection of conversations with seventeen top medical experts that makes the case for vegetarianism/veganism as it has never been made before. A thorough yet concise guide to healthful eating.
- *The Caring Cook*, Janet Hunt (available from the Vegan Society, see above). Written specially for anyone new to cruelty-free cookery. Easy to use, full of tips, with recipes for everyday use and special occasions – and bargain priced.
- *Linda McCartney's Home Cooking*, Linda McCartney and Peter Cox (Bloomsbury 1989). Quick, easy and economical contemporary vegetarian recipes.
- *Alternatives to Factory Farming*, Paul Carnell (Earth Resources Research 1983). From deep-litter egg production to crateless veal, an examination of 'humane' ways to switch from the intensive animal agriculture that took hold after the Second World War.
- *Eat Green, Lose Weight*, Vernon Coleman (Angus & Robertson 1990).

Hunting

- *Outfoxed*, Michael Huskisson (available from the author at West Lodge, St James, Halesworth, Suffolk IP19 0HU).

- *The Politics of Hunting*, Richard Thomas (Gower 1983)
- *The Hunt and the Anti-Hunt*, Philip Windeatt (Pluto Press 1982). Interesting if only to see how others excuse themselves!
- *The Tradition of Stag Hunting on Exmoor*, the Devon and Somerset Residents' Association for Deer Protection (available from the League Against Cruel Sports, 83–87 Union Street, London SE1 1SG, price £2.)

Wool
- *Pulling the Wool*, Christine Townend (Hale and Iremonger, Sydney, Australia, 1985).

Seaworld
- *The Magic of Dolphins*, Horace Dobbs (Lutterworth Press 1990). The famous 'dolphin man' tells about encounters he's had with dolphin friends, and his concern for their future.
- *Whale Nation*, Heathcote Williams (Jonathan Cape 1988). Destined to become a classic, this moving combination of poetry and facts is now out in paperback. (See also his book, *Sacred Elephant*.)

Animals in Captivity
- *The Rose-Tinted Menagerie*, William Johnson (Heretic Books 1990). A disturbing and very thorough investigation into circuses, zoos and dolphinaria around the world.

Feminism
- *The Sexual Politics of Meat*, Carol J. Adams (Polity Press 1990). Thought-provoking book that links animal rights and those of women.

Fiction
- *The Plague Dogs*, Richard Adams (Penguin Books 1978). Two dogs escape from a laboratory where they have been horribly tortured. Also a film (ask at video stores).
- *Doctor Rat*, William Kotzwinkle (Corgi Books 1977). A witty but gruesome tale of animals in a laboratory.
- *Hackenfeller's Ape*, Brigid Brophy (Allison & Busby 1979). A novel about a scientist who fights to save a monkey from

being shot into space. Compels readers to ponder the philosophical premises on which we base our discriminations against others.

- *I want to go to Moscow*, Maureen Duffy (Methuen 1986). Originally published in the early 1970s, this thriller predicted ALF-type activities for animal rights.
- *Space Trap*, Monica Hughes (Magnet 1984, to be reprinted). Science fiction with a message about communication between all intelligent beings.

Religion
- *The Moral Status of Animals*, Steven R.L. Clark (Oxford University Press 1977).
- *Christianity and the Rights of Animals*, Andrew Linzey (SPCK 1987).

Companion Animals
- *In the Company of Animals*, James Serpell (Basil Blackwell 1986). A discussion of the sociological implications of how people treat their animal companions.
- *Mother Knows Best*, Carol Lea Benjamin (Howell, New York, 1985). Dog-training designed to mimic that of canine mothers, using body language and games and spoken words, and emphasising dogs' natural behaviour.

Cruelty-free Living
- *Herbal Cosmetics*, Camilla Hepper (Thorsons 1987). All natural products, including recipes for home-made cosmetics.
- *The Cruelty Free Shopper*, Lis Howlett (Bloomsbury 1989). A comprehensive list of vegan food, cosmetics, toiletries and household products.

Children
- *Some People Don't Eat Meat*, Jane Inglis (Oakroyd, Potters Bar, Herts.). A clear and simple explanation of the reasons for not eating meat, and how to become a vegetarian (age 5 to 10).
- *Mrs Frisby and the Rats of NIMH*, Robert O'Brien (Puffin 1975). A well-wrought and refreshingly unsentimental tale of rats and mice escaping from a laboratory (age 10 and over).

- Classics: *Black Beauty, Charlotte's Web, The Hundred and One Dalmatians, The Story of Ferdinand,* and *Blueberries for Sal* (available from many publishers and libraries).

Magazines
- *Liberator* (BUAV, 16a Crane Grove, London N7 8LB).
- *The Vegetarian* (Vegetarian Society (UK) Ltd., Parkdale, Dunham Road, Altrincham, Cheshire WA14 4QG).
- *Greenscene* (Vegetarian Society's magazine for under 16s).
- *The Vegan* (Vegan Society, 7 Battle Road, St Leonards-on-Sea, East Sussex TN37 7AA).
- *Outrage* (Animal Aid, 7 Castle Street, Tonbridge, Kent TN9 1BH).
- *Compassion* (Beauty Without Cruelty, 57 King Henry's Walk, London N1 4NH).
- *BBC Wildlife Magazine* (from newsagents everywhere).

8
ACTIVISM ON THE JOB

The fate of animals is of greater importance to me than the fear of appearing ridiculous; it is indissolubly connected with the fate of men.

EMILE ZOLA

THE PROBLEM
For most of us, roughly 2,000–3,000 hours annually (80,000–120,000 hours in a professional lifetime!) are spent at work – that's equal to nine to fourteen uninterrupted years of our lives. It's comforting to know that, at the office and 'in the field', there are hundreds of ways to help the animals.

THE SOLUTION

Singers sing about animals, writers write about animals, and teachers teach about animals. No matter what you do, you can be an activist. David, whose job takes him around the country, leaves animals rights leaflets and literature in hotel rooms. Beryl, who works at a greengrocers, has an arrangement with the boss that she will deliver any left-overs to a local wildlife sanctuary.

- See if your employer has a 'matching funds programme' through which your company doubles employees' donations to favourite charities. If not, suggest the idea.

- If you have a staff cafeteria or dining room, ask the management to feature vegetarian options (and to get rid of veal!). The Vegetarian Society (Parkdale, Dunham Road, Altrincham, Cheshire WA14 4QG) have a *Choice* campaign which gives full information on providing vegetarian food in such establishments, including how to balance nutrients and menu planning. Recipes are also available. Suggest that the head of catering contacts them – or cut corners and do it yourself on behalf of your company. Get the support of other employees to show that healthful meals are in demand and would be appreciated.

- Ask the stationery manager to talk to suppliers about replacing office products such as Gillette ('Papermate' and 'Flair') pens and ('Liquid Paper') correction fluid, as well as those from other companies that still test on animals, with cruelty-free office products such as Quill pens and Rotex correction fluid. Office computers use vast quantities of paper; by switching to recycled paper you will be helping to conserve trees essential to the lives of birds and other animals. The same with loo paper. Suggest also that soap in the loos comes from companies on the cruelty-free list, and that it is labelled as such to show visitors and staff.

- When you've finished reading your animal protection magazines and literature, bring them to work for others to look through. Set up a rack in common areas such as lounges and dining rooms.

- Wear a badge to work. Let colleagues know how you feel about cruelty-free living, and other animal issues.

- If your office or company organises social events, invite an animal protection professional to show a film, give a talk, or lead or be part of a seminar or panel discussion.
- Display an animal rights poster near your desk or work station as a conversation starter and thought provoker.
- Get on food and organising committees to ensure that all staff parties and picnics have vegetarian and vegan options. Try suggesting a completely vegetarian event to show colleagues just how good such food can taste! Help choose convention sites and hotels to ensure vegetarian food will be available. Make known your objections to the idea of using furs or other offensive prizes as staff incentives, always suggesting alternatives.
- Post carriers can distribute free fact sheets and pamphlets on their routes.
- If you work in or for a shopping arcade, building company, car dealership, school or college, make sure the establishment or institution has a policy to use harmless alternatives to glue or other kinds of mousetrap, and never to institute a pigeon or rodent poisoning programme or to use harmful lawn chemicals. Make sure animal acts or exhibits are banned. Campaign for an electronic security system rather than guard dogs (who are usually grossly mistreated and deprived ex-companion animals).

9

SAFEGUARD YOUR ANIMAL FRIEND

Not to hurt our humble brethren is our first duty to them, but to stop there is not enough. We have a higher mission – to be of service to them wherever they require it.

FRANCIS OF ASSISI (1181–1220), quoted in the *Life* by St Bonaventura

THE PROBLEM

Companion animals are vulnerable to theft and human mischief. It is a known fact that thieves can make a living cruising neighbourhoods for dogs and cats they sell to laboratories for vivisection, to guard dog companies or for dog-fighting. Some are sold as food; eating cats and dogs is as common a practice in many parts of the world as Britain's cow, chicken and pig slaughter. Eight hundred cats' paws were found in a rubbish tip in Manchester, police suspecting they belonged to stolen cats whose meat and/or fur were sold.

Did you Know?

● More than 10 million households in Britain 'own' an animal including over 6 million dogs and 6 million cats, yet not all these people are responsible guardians. It is estimated that half a million dogs are allowed to roam the streets and countryside every day. These are what are known as 'latchkey' dogs – dogs turned out on to the streets because their owners are busy, disinterested, or have to go out to work. Most of the dogs return in the evening, but many of them don't. The poor unfortunates who just wander off (especially likely if they have not been spayed or neutered) make especially easy pickings for thieves.

● Officially the law makes no provision for missing cats. The police are not bound even to log details of losses. (Stolen cats are a different matter, but you must give very good reasons for believing your cat has actually been stolen!) This means that estimated losses cannot be verified. Cats, however, do not usually wander further than a precise territory unless searching for food or a mate; and as most domesticated cats are reasonably well fed, and the majority are spayed, it is unlikely that most of those who go missing have simply wandered off. In fact, National Petwatch have evidence clearly suggesting that theft is the main cause of cat losses in the UK.

● The cat fur trade is huge: many black market pelts are sent abroad, most of them probably to Germany where the shortage of pelts brought about by CITES (the Convention on International Trade in Endangered Species) and restrictions on seal-culling makes them especially valuable for the making of fashion garments and cuddly toys.

THE SOLUTION

Take measures to safeguard your companion animals. Here's how:

● Be vigilant. Never leave dogs unsupervised in a garden or yard, or chained or tied up alone. Dogs left unattended in cars are a favourite target for thieves. Cats, especially those living in cities, should not be allowed to wander. As the majority of stolen cats are snatched at night, get into a routine of feeding yours late in the evening, then lock the cat flap.

● Always have current photographs of your companion animals, in case they go missing.

● All dogs should wear a disc giving name, address and phone number. Join the National Canine Defence League, and you will be given a special disc that helps ensure your dog is given prompt and maybe life-saving treatment should he be injured whilst away from you (available to non-members for a fee). Fasten this to a standard nylon (not leather) collar; check for sizing by fitting two fingers comfortably between the collar and the neck. Have a reserve disc handy in case the first one gets lost or damaged.

● Certainly lost cats have a better chance of being returned to their guardians if wearing identification. On the other hand, there are numerous reports of problems caused by rigid collars (not just from strangulation; a recent report tells of a cat whose leg was trapped in the collar). Some rigid collars also make it easier for a thief to catch and restrain a cat. If you do choose to use one, use an easy-to-replace piece of sewing elastic and print your name, address and phone number on it in indelible ink. Inexpensive non-leather safety release collars can be purchased from Ann James, 4 Green Street, Wollaston, Northants NN9 7RA (RSPCA and Cats Protection League approved).

• As a means of permanent identification, the Battersea Dogs Home are using microchips which are inserted into the scruff of the neck, a procedure which is fairly painless and should make it easy to keep track of a dog's details (though the system is not yet without its problems). If interested, check with your local vet.

• *Never, never* advertise puppies, kittens or any animal as 'FREE TO A GOOD HOME'. This is just the kind of advertisement that saves unscrupulous dealers a lot of time and work! Most vets will be happy to put up a notice for you, or may even know of someone who (for example) has recently lost an other-than-human friend and has space in home and heart for a new one. For advice on this or other problems contact one of these organisations:

○ National Canine Defence League, 1 Pratt Mews, London NW1 0AD. As well as the disc mentioned above, the league has 'Lost Dog Packs' that include a special poster (with room for a photo) for you to put in shop windows and other prominent places. Also runs a scheme to ensure your dog is cared for in the event of your being in hospital or dying.

○ Cats Protection League, 17 King's Road, Horsham, West Sussex RH13 5PP. In addition to taking in strays, the league provides a number of free pamphlets and leaflets on various subjects ranging from 'Cats and Babies' to dealing with parasites. Also campaigns on relevant subjects; a recent petition presented to Parliament was on the tightening up of laws on the sale of airguns (these are frequently used on cats).

O RSPCA, The Causeway, Horsham, West Sussex RH12 1HG. At present there is no compulsory registration scheme for dogs, though the RSPCA strongly believes that such a scheme would help prevent much of the cruelty to dogs, and continues to campaign for one to be made law. If you agree – or would simply like to know more – contact the RSPCA.

O National Petwatch, P.O. Box 16, Brighouse, West Yorkshire HD6 1DS. Has a national network of missing cats and dogs bureaux offering practical advice and assistance to anyone whose friend has disappeared. Collects information and data on missing animals, the majority of whom it believes are stolen. Campaigns to make the public aware of this fact and therefore more vigilant.

• If your friend goes missing:

O Scour the neighbourhood, check the 'Lost and Found' section of your newspapers, visit shelters daily. Question anyone delivering post or newspapers, local children and neighbours for information.

O Call out at night when it's quiet. Check behind sheds and garages, under parked cars and bushes. Frightened animals will get as far as possible away from people: check any nearby wasteland and empty houses.

O Spray-paint big, simple messages on scrap plywood and place them at intersections so that drivers can't miss them. Keep it simple, e.g., BLACK DOG LOST, CALL 123 4567. Offering a reward often helps. Make sure someone is home to take phone calls, or if you have an answering machine, make sure callers know that you are the one looking for the BLACK DOG.

O Contact all local vets, and leave cards in shops and on bulletin boards. No matter what shelters tell you over the telephone, go there personally no less than once a day and be sure to show the workers photos of the lost animal. Also check with dustmen and road-sweepers for information about any dead animals.

○ If you have recently moved, leave notices with neighbours in the old area and check with animal shelters there, or send a reliable friend or relative who knows the missing animal to look for her or him.

○ Put an ad in the 'Lost and Found' section of local and community papers, and distribute 'Have you seen . . .?' notes door-to-door. Many local radio stations now have a 'lost animal' spot – contact them.

○ Keep looking! Missing animals have been reunited with persistent humans after many months of searching.

10

DOGS AND CATS GO VEGETARIAN

The US Department of Agriculture uses the term '4-D' to indicate flesh that's considered unfit for human consumption. The 'D's; are: dead, dying, disabled, and diseased. In all but a few states, flesh from 4-D animals can be sold to pet food manufacturers . . . [Jim] Mason and [Peter] Singer report an average of 15 million pounds of cancerous tissues a year (added to slaughterhouse reject piles) much of which is rendered into 'by-products' on pet food labels.
BARBARA LYNN PEDEN, *Dogs and Cats Go Vegetarian*

THE PROBLEM

In 1989 we spent some £800 million on tinned 'pet food' for our dogs and cats. These – made up of organ meats, veins, even the skin between pigs' ears and chickens' toes – contribute to the suffering of both companion and farm animals. Most vegetarians recognise that many 'pet food' ingredients come from the very same slaughterhouses that violently produce flesh intended for human consumption, and that these foods generally consist of the waste products of the slaughter industry, including diseased, cancerous flesh marked 'unfit for human consumption', as well as growth hormones, antibiotics and other such chemicals. In Britain, cancer is a major cause of non-accidental death in cats and dogs and the second greatest in humans.

In the wild, dogs are omnivorous and cats carnivorous, so many people hesitate to provide these now domesticated species with a vegetarian or vegan diet. Of course, no one can argue that it is 'natural' for dogs and cats to live on a purely vegetarian diet, but neither is it 'natural' for these animals to be eating preslaughtered cows and pigs, or even living in our homes. Thanks to the research and work of Barbara Lynn Peden and others, we now know that many dogs and cats can do very well on a nutritionally sound vegetarian, or even vegan, diet.

THE SOLUTION

- For cats, we recommend Vegepet supplements, which come in two forms: 'Vegekit' for kittens and 'Vegecat' for cats over the age of ten months. These are available from Katz Go Vegan (see address below), and come with complete instructions and recommended recipes such as:

CHICKPEA CAT CHOW (Peden)

75g (2½ oz) sprouted chickpeas
1½ tbsp nutritional yeast powder
1 tbsp chopped or grated vegetables
1 tbsp oil
½ tsp Vegecat
⅓ tsp soy sauce

Mash well together, put into an airtight container, refrigerate and use as needed.

- Cats are more likely to need extra incentives to eat unfamiliar foods than are dogs. Peden provides the following 'helpful hints': use textured vegetable protein with simulated flesh flavour (e.g. 'beef mince', available from wholefood and healthfood stores); serve the food warm; sprinkle nutritional yeast on top; temporarily add soy milk, avocado,

departure, and carry water for rest stops. Install shade blinds on windows, and try to never leave animals unattended in parked cars. If you must, make sure doors are locked and that there is adequate ventilation, especially in summer – a grid or grill across the window is a must (cars can very quickly turn into ovens once the sun gets on to them, with results that are too often fatal). And hurry back to your friend!

- When travelling by car with a cat, confine her or him in a sturdy, well-ventilated carrier big enough for her or him to stand up and turn around in comfortably. Line it with a towel, and if possible put in a tiny litter tray. The carrier should have a door that lets you see in and lets your friend see both you and the inside of the car, but blocks out views of oncoming cars and flashing lights, which can be frightening. If possible, secure the carrier to the seat with a belt. Open the carrier several days before the trip and let the cat get used to it (try a little catnip).

    Note: a cardboard box with holes punched into it is dangerous because cats can often squeeze out, and the box provides almost no protection in an accident.

- Dogs can eigher be put in sturdy travel kennels or ride unrestrained. Stay alert to prevent possible escapes. Both the National Canine Defence League (1 Pratt Mews, London NW1 0AD) and the Humane Research Trust, (Brook House, 29 Bramhall Lane, South, Bramhall, Cheshire SK7 2DN) sell easy-to-fit dog harnesses that work in much the same way as a seat belt. And don't forget to stop and walk your dog often!

Once You've Arrived

- *Camping*: if you enjoy camping and like to get well away from everyone you should have no problems. (Except to watch out for the sheep and cattle who may well find your tent or caravan intriguing; do keep your dog under control or he or she may be shot, and quite legally too!) Some campsites accept dogs, others don't. Most of them insist that dogs are kept on a lead while on their grounds. If you intend to book in advance, do make sure your friend will be welcome.

- Finding lodgings that will take animal companions is not difficult, even though many of the bigger hotels are reluctant to do so, especially in high season. (An exception is the huge Consort Hotels Group which actually makes a feature of inviting people to bring their dogs to selected hotels around the country. Ring (0904) 643151 for details.) Again, check before making any bookings. An invaluable little book is *Pets Welcome* (FHG Publications, price £2.50), which is updated each year, and lists guest houses, hotels and self-catering establishments that are happy for you to bring your friend.

- Walking your dogs may well be one of the most enjoyable aspects of holidaying together, but when in an unfamiliar area, do take care, both for their sake and for that of others. Keep them on leads unless you are sure there will be no problems; look out for and take note of warning signs. The National Trust (NT) has fifty-seven nature reserves and over 400 designated 'Sites of Special Scientific Interest', most of which allow dogs to run free (but under control, of course!), except when land has been let to farmers who may have animals grazing. If, while on a reserve, you want to visit any of the National Trust homes, check in advance whether or not dogs are allowed. *The National Trust Family Handbook* (from NT shops around the country, price £3.50) gives details. Nowadays many of the most popular beaches will be closed to dogs in the summer. *The Good Beach Guide* (Ebury Press updated each year), details over 180 of them, and will warn you of such restrictions.

Staying Behind

- Your animal companions love you and will miss you, so greet and leave them with this foremost in your mind. Always remember to say goodbye. Use a kind 'stay' look directed into your friend's eyes and say, very reassuringly and firmly, 'I'll be back.' When you return, always say, *first* thing, 'I'm back.' The idea that your absence will not be forever is reinforced in this simple way.
- Keep your dogs or cats safely at home, rather than boarding them out with strangers. There's a lot to be said for familiar surroundings – they are generally the safest and least stressful. Try to find a responsible (adult) friend or relative to stay at your home, or to call in *at least* three times a day to

keep an eye on the animals and tend to their needs (i.e. allow them to relieve themselves). Even if there are ample provisions, accidents happen and someone should make safety checks often. If you can't find someone you know and trust, consider a 'pet-sitting' service that has several verifiable and reliable references from a vet, or other satisfied client).

- Make sure the chosen caretaker has all the information she or he may need about your animal's likes, dislikes, needs and funny little ways! Leave important phone numbers by the telephone, including a twenty-four-hour veterinary surgery, and a number at which you can be reached.

- If you *must* board, choose very carefully. Though some shelters do also take short-term boarders, your dog or cat might find the distress of other animals upsetting. This does not mean that commercial boarding kennels are necessarily guaranteed to be a better bet – some of them can be little shops of horrors. Animal welfare inspectors have frightening stories to tell, such as animals stacked in crates during peak boarding seasons, and families returning home to find that their friends had 'escaped'. Ask around. References from satisfied customers are a good starting point. Then go and look around any kennels you are considering. Those that take pride in their premises and work will be only too happy to invite you in. Take note of standards of cleanliness, how relaxed the dogs and cats seem, how they react to the person who is showing you around. If you can take your animal along at the same time and introduce him or her to the kennel staff, even better. If you find one you especially like do remember to book in advance. The best places are likely to be popular.

12

OBJECTING TO DISSECTING

What are we doing when we brainwash children in schools to cut open their fellow animals? Are we dangerously de-sensitising them? Some of the most warped and blunted people I know are those who have gone through prolonged trainings of this sort.

RICHARD D. RYDER, from the Proceedings of the Symposium held by the Humane Education Council at Sussex University, 1980

If [man] is not to stifle human feelings, he must practise kindness towards animals, for he who is cruel to animals becomes hard also in his dealings with men. We can judge the heart of man by his treatment of animals.

IMMANUEL KANT, *Lectures on Ethics*

I . . . know that it was a waste of time for me to take about twenty-three years to be able to recognise a toad as an important entity and not merely an adjunct to other life, including my own.

M.F.K. FISCHER, *A Cordiall Water*

THE PROBLEM

In the 1970s, some 200,000 rats, frogs, mice, hamsters, gerbils, other animals and insects were dissected annually in British schools as an integral part of biology and zoology courses. Over recent years the numbers have diminished as students and teachers have begun to question not just the value of this exercise, but the ethics; to ask if the study of life should revolve around the death of other-than-humans. Their concern has meant that most examining boards no longer make dissection compulsory, offering alternatives instead (the London Examination Board being the first to remove dissection totally from the A-level biology syllabus). Still, though, it takes courage and determination to stand up in class and refuse to do something everyone else may be doing, especially if you are teased for being 'soft'; but there may well be others who will be only too happy to join you, once the stand has been made.

THE SOLUTION

Help to stop suffering in the school lab by refusing to dissect, and encouraging others to do the same. Here is the way to go about it:

- Know your rights. At GSCE-level dissection is not compulsory. At A-level some examination boards do insist on dissection, though they may provide an alternative or give you special consideration. Start by telling your teacher politely but firmly that you are not prepared to dissect. If possible, enlist the support of your parents (you have to be educated in accordance with your parents' wishes); they should speak to your teacher, school governors and – if necessary – the local council on your behalf.
- Animal Aid Youth Group has lots of good advice for young people concerned about dissection. Contact them for their information pack, and with any specific questions which they will do their best to answer.
- Take comfort from others. Despite the fact that experiments on living animals in universities and polytechnics have again increased over the last decade, the National Union of Students recently launched a campaign to defend the right of any science undergraduate to refuse to carry out work on animals. They argue that exercises such as studying the effects of drugs on the exposed and beating heart of a frog whose nervous system has been destroyed by a needle in the base of the skull are unjustified, especially with so much alternative material now widely available. In 1987 the Argentinian government banned dissection in schools, saying that 'it is necessary to promote knowledge . . . in a way consistent with respect and reverence for all forms of life'.
- Find out about alternatives. There are a number of these now available, including computer simulations (that allow the 'frog' to be put back together again and hop from the screen!), films, videos, specially made models. Ask your

teacher to contact the British Union for the Abolition of Vivisection (BUAV) for a list of suppliers. BUAV will also give details of examination board requirements, including what will be expected from you on university courses. The Humane Research Trust has an education pack that gives an alternative approach to studying animals (without dissection or experiments), including ten study cards giving masses of information to encourage discussion and debate.

- Get other students to join you. Start by distributing leaflets about dissection to them, and be ready to answer any questions they may have. Write letters to your school newspaper, or an article on how you personally feel about dissection. Get signatures on your Students Charter; make up your own petition form, or get one from the National Anti-Vivisection Society (NAVS) who will also give help or advice about getting the charter adopted at your college/university.

- If you aren't getting a positive response from your school, you may want to contact the National Council for Civil Liberties who have pledged to support students' basic right to refuse to participate in dissection without penalty. You could also try calling local TV and radio stations to let them know what is happening.

- Remember: animals delivered dead to classrooms did not die of natural causes. They were killed, usually by the crudest and cheapest methods, only because someone could make money selling their bodies. By cutting off the demand, cutting up animals will end.

RESOURCES

- Animal Aid Youth Group, 7 Castle Street, Tonbridge, Kent TN9 1BH; tel. (0732) 364546.
- British Union for the Abolition of Vivisection (BUAV), 16a Crane Grove, Islington, London N7 8LB; tel. (071) 700 4888.
- Humane Research Trust, Brook House, 29 Bramhall Lane South, Bramhall, Cheshire SK7 2DN; tel. (061) 439 8041.
- National Anti-Vivisection Society (NAVS), 261 Goldhawk Road, London W12 9PE; tel. (081) 846 9777.

- National Council for Civil Liberties, 21 Tabard Street, London SE1 4LA,
- RSPCA, Education Department, The Causeway, Horsham, West Sussex RH12 1HG; tel. (0403) 64181. Has a range of guides including *Alternatives to Dissection*.

13

GREAT-GRANDMA KNEW BEST

Purge me with hyssop, and I shall be clean: wash me, and I shall be whiter than snow.

Psalm 51:7

THE PROBLEM

Household products sold in stores can involve a variety of hidden hazards, ranging from potentially and known dangerous ingredients to environmentally destructive packaging. Commerically prepared cleaners, for example, may contain chemicals that can cause cancer, respiratory problems, or other illnesses in humans and companion animals.

Many commercial detergents also contain phosphates that end up in animals' river and stream homes. Even small amounts of them can cause huge increases in the growth of algae. When the algae die, micro-organisms use up the water's oxygen, leaving untold numbers of fish, crustaceans, and other aquatic animals to suffocate.

THE 'SOLUTION'

Dozens of safe and effective home recipes can be concocted from substances as inexpensive as bicarbonate of soda and vinegar. Here are some suggestions:

Cleansers

Cooking utensils: Let pots and pans soak in bicarbonate of soda solution before washing.

Copper cleaner: Use a paste of lemon juice, salt, and flour; or rub vinegar and salt into the copper.

Furniture polish: Mix three parts olive oil and one part vinegar, or one part lemon juice and two parts vegetable oil. Use a soft cloth.

General cleaner: Mix bicarbonate of soda with a small amount of water.

Glass cleaner: White vinegar and water.

Household cleaner: Three tablespoons of bicarbonate of soda mixed into 2 pints of warm water.

Linoleum floor cleaner: One cup of white vinegar mixed with two gallons of water to wash, soda water to polish.

Mildew remover: Lemon juice or white vinegar and salt.

Stain remover, toilet bowl cleaner: Vinegar.

Wine/coffee stains: Blot the fresh spill with a cloth soaked with soda water.

Insect Repellents

Ant control: Pour a line of cream of tartar at the place where ants enter the house – they will not cross it.

Ant repellent: Wash countertops, cupboards and floors with equal parts vinegar and water.

Cockroach repellent: Place whole bay leaves in several locations around kitchen.

Flea and tick repellent: Feed brewer's yeast and garlic tablets to companion animals. Place herbs, such as fennel, rue, pennyroyal and rosemary, eucalyptus seeds and leaves, or cedar chips where the animal sleeps to repel fleas. Make daily use of a flea comb.

Mosquito repellent: Add brewer's yeast to food or take it in tablet form daily during the summer months.

Mothballs: Place cedar chips around clothes. Dried lavender can be made into sachets and placed in drawers and closets.

Miscellaneous

Air freshener: Leave an opened box of bicarbonate of soda in the

room, or add cloves and cinnamon to boiling water and simmer.
Scent the house with fresh flowers or herbs, or open windows
(in the winter, for about fifteen minutes every morning).

Kitchen sink drain: Prevent clogging by flushing the drain weekly
with about a gallon of boiling water. If clogged, pour half a cup
of bicarbonate of soda, then half a cup of vinegar down the
drain and cover it tightly for about a minute. Also, don't forget
the traditionally effective plunger.

Odour remover (spills and accidents): On carpet or furniture, blot the
fresh stain with a cloth soaked with cider vinegar.

Water softener: A quarter of a cup of vinegar in the final rinse.

14

CREATE A BACKGARDEN SANCTUARY

> I'm sure I've been a toad, one time or another. With bats,
> weasels, worms . . . I rejoice in the kinship. Even the
> caterpillar I can love, and the various vermin.
>   THEODORE ROETHKE, from 'Slug'

THE PROBLEM

We cause our wild animal neighbours far more trouble than
they cause us, as each day we invade thousands of acres of their
territory and demolish their homes. Where their feeding and
nesting grounds once thrived, are now our barren, crew-cut
lawns. Hedges they used as homes are replaced with neat
wooden fences. Wild flowers are treated as weeds.

We are the losers. As a direct result of our destructive ways
butterflies, once so common, are rarely seen in some areas; the

common frog is uncommon; boxing hares – one of the first signs of spring – are seen only by the very lucky few.

If, however, you have access to a garden or patch of land, however small, you can do something positive to help the survival of many species of animals, insects and birds.

THE SOLUTION

Here are some ways to help wild animals maintain their precious homes:

- Don't use pesticides in your garden. In addition to polluting the groundwater, lawn chemicals can endanger the songbird population by contaminating the worms they eat. No pesticide is safe for birds. Even those designed for the home will poison birds' water and food supplies.
- Leave a good part of your garden natural, with bushes and groundcover. The more diverse your bushes, seeds and berries, the greater variety of birds and small mammals you will attract and nurture. Encourage or even plant wild flowers; a few enlightened companies are selling seeds! Stinging nettles will help encourage butterflies; they are also very fond of buddleias (sometimes called 'the butterfly bush').
- Starting a small pond is easier than you may think. If there's space, do consider making one to help our fast-disappearing amphibians. Position it somewhere quiet, preferably not under trees (and away from young children for the sake of the pond's inhabitants as well as the children!). Edge it with water plants, add water lilies to offer shelter. The news will soon spread.
- Our preoccupation with tidying up means that as soon as a tree falls (or becomes damaged or diseased, and therefore less than perfect) we remove it. Yet dead wood is ecological gold and crucial to kicking our pesticide habit. More than 150 species of birds and animals live in dead trees and/or feed on the insects there. Top off, rather than chop down, dead trees twelve inches or more in diameter. Leave tree stumps, fat dead logs, woody debris and underbush, all of which are precious to wildlife. Before cutting any wood, check for nests and dens.

- Keep water in a birdbath all year round, using a heating element to keep it from freezing in winter; during harsh weather many birds die not from starvation but thirst. A deeper pan would be appreciated for bathing purposes. Be sure neither is placed too close to a bush or other cover where a cat might hide.
- Build a bat house. There is no guarantee you will get takers, but as an increasing number of trees are felled, bats will be on the lookout for any suitable home. A bat consumes 3,000 or more mosquitoes and other insects nightly; in tropical rain-forests they are responsible for up to 95 per cent of the seed dispersal essential to regeneration. They don't get in your hair either! For help and advice contact your local group of batophiles (address from the Vincent Wildlife Trust, Baltic Exchange Buildings, 21 Ebury Street, London EC3A 5AU).
- It's probably best not to encourage badgers and foxes into your garden, though if one should get the habit of calling in – especially when food supplies are scarce – do put out some snack. (Urban foxes are, in fact, one of the survival success stories of recent times, finding life in the city a lot easier than life in their increasingly hostile natural environment!) Squirrels make amusing visitors; they'll usually help them-selves to the birds' nuts if they are really hungry. Hedgehogs are sadly now very scarce in much of the country, killed off by fast cars, litter and slug pellets. Should you be lucky enough to have one in your garden and feel he needs food, it's said hedgehogs enjoy peanut butter sandwiches! In hot weather, or extreme cold, do also put out some water for your visitor.

Uninvited visitors? Some ideas for dealing with them:
- To remove less-than-welcome visitors to your home, do *not* call out the local council. The service they offer involves poisoning rats and mice, spraying (with lethal chemicals) wasps, cockroaches and other insects. Keeping your home clean and blocking off potential entry spots should help prevent the problem in the first place. But if not, there are kinder ways to solve the problem.
- If bats should enter your house, turn off all lights and open

the doors and windows. If they still don't leave, they can be caught in a large jar or net and released outside. Wear gloves, since a frightened bat may bite. Then seal the point of entry, which may be as narrow as 3/8"!

- Found birds or other small animals with a nest of young in the attic, or another unused part of the house? If they are doing no significant harm, leave the family alone for a few weeks until the youngsters are grown. They will probably then move out on their own.

- Wasps also like to build their nests in attics or sheds. Though beneficial in many ways, wasps can be a nuisance when around food, and may even sting. (Avoid attracting them to you by not wearing perfumes, hair spray, brightly coloured or patterned clothes). You may be able to encourage them to leave their nest by putting out saucers filled with a mixture of water and ammonia (they hate the smell). If not, the best thing is to shut off from the rest of the house the area in which the nest is situated, and leave it until the cold weather. Wasps do not re-use their nests, so in the winter remove it and seal up any possible points of entry so that next spring they will find a more suitable place.

RESOURCES

- Two very good (but possibly out-of-date books) are *The Backgarden Wildlife Sanctuary Book* by Ron Wilson (Astragal Books 1979) and *Nature On Your Side* by Greet Buchner and Fieke Hoogvelt (Pan 1978). Look out for them in bargain bookshops or at jumbles, or see if your library can get them for you.

- Also very useful: *How to Make a Wildlife Garden* by Chris Baines (Elm Tree Books 1985).

- *Something in a Cardboard Box* by Les Stocker (Chatto and Windus 1989) tells the inspiring story of the Wildlife Hospital Trust which was started by Les and Sue Stocker in their own back garden. Delightful reading, plus tips on caring for wildlife and birds in your back garden.

- Royal Society for the Protection of Birds (RSPB), The Lodge, Sandy, Bedfordshire SG19 2DL. Lots of information on how to help birds; also sells bird tables and other useful items.

- British Hedgehog Preservation Society, Knowbury House, Knowbury, Ludlow, Shropshire SY8 3LQ.

15

OUT OF SIGHT . . .

Imagine.

JOHN LENNON.

THE PROBLEM

Planet Earth is fighting for survival. As the population increases at the rate of nearly 200 people every minute (300 born, 100 die) space becomes more limited, the air more polluted, water and food commodities to be fought over. Animals, birds and fish, our fellow-travellers through the universe, feel enormous pressure as humans demand their space to live in, their oceans to dump waste in, their bodies to eat and to make car seat covers, face creams and glue for our stamps. They have become just another resource to help us survive that much longer.

The horror of the effect this is having on other-than-humans is hard to imagine. and that is why it is allowed to happen. We all have a tendency to block out unpleasant facts, to control our imaginations, to curb feelings that others might describe as over-emotional. Empathising has become a weakness, compassion an indulgence. Yet if more people stopped to think, not just about animals but about how the British way of life directly affects them, maybe things would be a little better for the animals.

On the surface, the recent 'green' revolution appears to be a good thing. At least people are now thinking before they buy. The trouble is that industry has jumped on to the bandwagon and is promoting even non-green products as 'green': fur coats, nuclear fuel, weedkiller, new models of cars, all have been promoted with claims that they are 'environment friendly'. How can the average person in the street begin to know what is what? How can we judge who is telling the truth? We know that by eating hamburgers we are destroying the rainforests; by using a certain spray on our hair we are destroying the ozone layer – but is eating cheese any better? What about hair gel?

Consumer Facts

- Getting frozen orange juice to the consumer takes four times the energy and several times the packaging of providing fresh oranges. Potato chip production takes four times the energy budget of potatoes.
- In the USA the typical mouthful of food travels 1,300 miles from farm to dinner table. Travelling by air consumes six and a half times as much energy per mile as travelling by the average car.
- The world's three largest cash crops are tea, coffee and cocoa, all products we can easily do without (in fact, tea and coffee are actually harmful to us). Yet in order that they might be produced in amounts to satisfy a worldwide demand, we allow vast areas of fertile land to be used, the plants are treated with tonnes of chemicals, and the final products are then transported across the world thus using fuel and polluting the air.
- Few of the products we buy are made in Britain. Check next time you are in a department store, or even in your own home. Hi-fi systems and cars come from Japan, cooking utensils from France, writing paper from Germany, cameras from Russia. We also make most of these products in Britain – and send them overseas.
- Economic growth depends on a successful import/export balance. We are encouraged to be consumers. Yet the movement of commodities – food, and other products – around the world is a major cause of the death of millions of other-than-humans each year.
- Though few of us have seen an endangered species animal in the flesh, television, books and magazines have brought home to us their beauty and their plight. We want to help

them but don't know how. Money pours into funds to protect them from poaching, to preserve tiny scraps of forest that may be reserved for them. But though lack of space is one of the reasons many of them are becoming extinct, our extravagant way of life in the West is also responsible. We want mahogany for our toilet seats, breakfast orange juice from Spain, mangetout peas in winter. We want always to be able to drive down to the corner shop, and so more and more ships bring petrol to our garages, some of them having accidents at sea, their cargo polluting the waters and thereby killing birds, fish and sea mammals.

THE SOLUTION
- Use your imagination. Allow yourself to empathise with whales in the seas, with elephants being trapped in ever-smaller reserves, with orangutans in what is left of the forests of Borneo. Recognise that the trend for an increase in consumerism is directly related to the decrease in wildlife and resolve to do the one thing you can do to help them all: live more simply.
- Whenever you buy anything your choice affects the environment and every living creature who depends on it. Don't rush into purchase, especially of what are called 'consumer durables'; stop and ask yourself if you really want/need something, or whether you may be buying it for some other reason (such as to cheer yourself up, to impress someone, or because everyone else has one). Ask yourself what benefits you are going to get from it, how it is going to improve your life. By all means go ahead if you are sure, but you may well find you can go without quite happily. Economic growth has not benefited other-than-humans, only those who exploit them and their environment.
- Encourage others to stop and think before they buy. We have all been encouraged to equate spending with 'having a good time'. Maybe there are more creative ways you and your friends can find to enjoy yourselves!

RESOURCE
Get hold of *Green Pages* by John Button (Optima, revised edition

1990). This large and informative book covers all aspects of living with care and compassion, including cruelty-free eating. Encourages readers to re-evaluate their whole attitude to life, the planet and other-than-humans with a view to doing the minimum harm. Makes it all seem easy!

16

DEER EDITOR . . .

> 'Fool!' said my muse to me, 'look in thy heart, and write.'
> SIR PHILLIP SIDNEY (1554—86)

THE POWER OF THE PEN

With just a pen and paper, you can be a strong advocate for animals. Members of Parliament receive thousands of letters every week on a wide variety of subjects relating to animal abuse; for example, the impending creation in 1992 of a 'free market' for all European Community member states, and the disastrous effect this is likely to have on animals, has resulted in petitions arriving at the House of Commons every day.

Letter-writing campaigns aimed at businesses have helped prompt companies to stop selling furs (Harrods, for example), and others (such as Avon, Revlon, Crabtree & Evelyn and Benetton) to stop testing cosmetics on animals. Effective letters to newspapers and magazines have encouraged countless people to reduce or eliminate their consumption of meat, or to take the children to a pantomime instead of to an animal circus. Letters put animal protection issues before the public, promoting both debate and action.

HOW TO WIELD IT
● Vow to write at least two letters a week: to your local MP

and Euro MP, to managing directors of companies making products that involve animal testing or ingredients, to food manufacturers and supermarkets, to the editors of newspapers and magazines. Keep an eye on local news and events for topical tie-ins.

- To make the best impression, type your letter. Otherwise, write legibly, both to encourage the recipient to read your letter and to ensure that he or she is able to read it. (Needless to say, an illegible message is no message at all.) Make your letter brief, stating your objective early on. Always be polite and never threaten. Avoid personal attacks and be sure of your facts. Check your letter for grammar and spelling mistakes (if necessary, ask a friend to read it over, and re-read it before posting).

- When writing letters to an editor, follow the publication's instructions concerning length and personal information (such as full name, address, or telephone number). A touch of humour may help your letter see publication, but don't sacrifice the tone of a strong, serious message just to draw a smile. If you have experience or a degree applicable to the subject, mentioning it can give your letter more credibility and authority – but don't be afraid to speak out for lack of initials after your name.

- When writing a letter of complaint to a business, go to the top. Explain your reasons for objecting to the company's particular practice; don't launch into a tirade of 'How can you be so cruel to innocent animals?' Most people just don't recognise the problem or have never stopped to think about it. Always suggest an alternative. If a radio station is giving away a fur coat, for instance, encourage the promotions manager to offer a trip or computer instead. Donnybrook Furlike Fashions of New York City has offered to replace real furs with *faux* furs in various US promotions. A bar in Maryland agreed to substitute wind-up toy turtles for real ones in a scheduled race because of a customer's concerns and suggestions.

Two sample letters to editors follow:

[Date]
Letters to the Editor
[Name of Newspaper]
[Address]

To the Editor:
Your article on cystic fibrosis patients ['Title of Article', date]
was touching, but I take exception to one parent's remark about
'vital' animal experiments. According to a representative of the
Cystic Fibrosis Foundation, 'No animal model exists for CF.'

Instead of pouring millions of pounds into making animals
sick, we should study CF, AIDS, cancer, heart disease, and
Alzheimer's non-invasively in human clinical studies, and we
should spend more on programmes that prevent disease – such
as AIDS education, dietary recommendations, and improved
prenatal care for the poor. Finally, we can use more relevant,
modern testing methods, such as epidemiological studies and
computer programmes that simulate human body functions.

We cannot realistically rely on animal tests to cure our ills,
and our blind faith exacts a high price – in funding, in lives and
in spirit.

Sincerely,
[Name, signed]
[Name, printed]
[Address]
[Phone number]

[Date]
Letters to the Editor
[Name of Newspaper]
[Address]

To the Editor:
The circus is in town, and advertisers are putting pressure on all
of us to buy tickets early and avoid long queues. Long queues for
what? To watch magnificent animals parade around in demeaning costumes, performing tricks that show none of the animals'

beauty or intelligence, but only the trainer's ability to dominate them.

The circus is a con – visitors spend lots of money on tickets, but the animals pay the greatest price.

They spend most of their lives in cages, are dragged not just from town to town but often overseas to venues as far away as South Africa and the Far East, are forced to perform awkward, demeaning, and unnatural tasks. For their sakes, this year avoid the circus with its whips, muzzles, bars, hooks, and chains. If you want to see animals in action, try bird-watching.

Sincerely,
[Name, signed]
[Name, printed]
[Address]
[Phone number]

17

SUPPORT YOUR LOCAL SHELTER

Knowing all truth is less than doing a little bit of good.
ALBERT SCHWEITZER, *The Thoughts of Albert Schweitzer*

THE PROBLEM AND THE POSSIBILITY

Just about every town has a shelter or sanctuary overflowing with dogs and cats waiting to be adopted or for their families to find them. Either way, these animals are often scared and confused, and even though you can't take them all home with you, they – and the people who run such places – would deeply appreciate your time, companionship, and resources.

Volunteering is a powerful tool for change. Helping minimise the impact of a seemingly overwhelming problem by making shelters more productive and less frightening places can be exceptionally fulfilling.

The Scope of Need

- The RSPCA has fifty-four local animal homes and rescue centres dotted around England and Wales. The Scottish Society for the Prevention of Cruelty to Animals has eight welfare centres plus other facilities for taking in animals. Each year, between them, they have millions of confused, unhappy, unwanted cats and dogs needing not just feeding and cleaning, but love and attention too. The Cats Protection League and the National Canine Defence League each handle thousands more.

- Sanctuaries for horses, ponies and donkeys are also plentiful, some of them taking in animals rescued from dreadful lives overseas. Apart from needing money and support, most of these places welcome the help of anyone who enjoys caring for equines. Check animal rights magazines for local addresses. Also, a magazine called *Equine Welfare* is on sale in most newsagents (or write to *Equine Welfare* Magazine, Finlay House, Southfield Road, Southam, Warwickshire CV33 0JH) and gives lots of information and contact points.

- In many areas, especially rural areas, there are private sanctuaries, most of them run on skeleton staffs and shoestring budgets. Some take in just one species, others are open to any other-than-human who needs treatment or just somewhere to live. Many cater especially for older unwanted animals, the idea behind them being that every animal deserves to grow old in peace and to die with dignity. Check your local telephone directory, newspapers, and animal rights magazines to see if there is one near you – you can be sure that if there is, your help will be welcome.

WHAT YOU CAN DO

- Offer to clean the cats' quarters and play chase-the-string with the felines. Give them each some lap time for scratches behind the ears. Bring a secure cat harness and take the cats out to stretch their legs on nice days.

- Donate blankets, newspapers, old towels, cat litter, and whatever else you can spare to make life more comfortable for the animals and less demanding on the shelter's funds. The more money your shelter saves on supplies, the more animals the facility can help.

- If your shelter has problems, resolve to help do something about them. Rather than blaming the usually stressed and overworked employees for inadequacies, get involved in improving things. Set up a 'Friends of the Shelter' committee: lobby, raise funds and awareness, write to newspapers and do whatever else it takes to improve conditions for animals there.

- Volunteer to 'ride along' on cruelty investigations to help load animals, carry crates, read the map, and provide an extra pair of hands. This can be harrowing and even dangerous work, so not all shelters will accept your offer. Others, however, may welcome it. Sharing can make a big difference to the morale of those who have to investigate cruelty charges, enforce animal protection and control laws, and confiscate abused animals. The experience will also help you to talk from first-hand knowledge about the importance of spaying and neutering, the reasons why companion animals must not roam unsupervised, and the ways in which animals suffer when neglected.

- Offer to take the dogs for walks one day a week, or as often as you can. Play tug-of-war, bring treats (unsalted peanuts are a favourite for many dogs and, in the shell, peanuts give them more of a challenge). Let the animals know that they are worth something by giving them individual attention.

- If it doesn't already, talk your local newspaper into running photos of the animals who are up for adoption at the shelter as a public service. Ask local television stations to help as well.

Wild Animals Need Help, Too

Volunteer to help local wildlife rehabilitators nurse injured wildlife back to good health and prepare them for release (your animal shelter should have names and numbers). Volunteer your time to help in the round-the-clock feeding of baby animals. Wildlife rehabilitation operations, like shelters, need soft bedding materials, newspapers, and other supplies. Most wildlife rehabilitation workers are good samaritans who aren't paid to help sick, injured, and orphaned wildlife get back on their feet, and they will welcome your assistance.

RESOURCES

Check your local telephone directory for shelters and sanctuaries in the area. Or, for details of local branches, contact the head offices of:

- RSPCA, The Causeway, Horsham, West Sussex RH12 1HG.
- Scottish Society for the Prevention of Cruelty to Animals, 19 Melville Street, Edinburgh EH3 7PL.
- Cats Protection League, 17 King's Road, Horsham, West Sussex RH13 5PP.
- National Canine Defence League, 1 Pratt Mews, London NW1 0AD.

18

BE FISH FRIENDLY

There are three prerequisites for angling,
A hook, a line, and a stinker.
JOHN BRYANT, *Fettered Kingdoms*

The first rule in sport used to be fairness. But where is the
fairness to the fish? Animals are not footballs or tennis
balls.
West German Judge, HORST BRINKMANN,
upon fining angling contest organisers
for cruelty, 1988

Now I can look at you in peace; I don't eat you any more.
FRANZ KAFKA (remark reportedly made
while admiring fish in an aquarium)

THE PROBLEM

Whether they're swimming in a little glass tank 'universe',
dodging plastic debris or crude oil, or struggling on a hook,
fishes around the world need our help.

'Pet' fishes are sold in pet shops, where they are often left in
crowded tanks that are cleaned infrequently. Goldfish are
spooned into polythene bags and given as prizes at fun fairs.
Fishes to be eaten are sold live in fish markets.

The capture of tropical saltwater species can wreak havoc on
the fishes' natural surroundings; commercial fishers in the
Philippines and other Pacific islands hire young children to dive
100 feet or more to bang heavy rocks on vulnerable, precious
coral reefs in order to chase fishes into nets, and others use
explosives to stun the fishes, making them easy to catch.

Fish Facts

- Around the world, close to 1,700 fishing vessels comb the
  oceans daily, leaving thousands of miles of plastic netting
  behind them, entangling and killing an estimated 100,000

marine mammals and at least a million birds annually. The boats dump rubbish as well, choking and poisoning sea dwellers.

- The risk of food poisoning from eating fish is twenty-five times greater than from eating beef and sixteen times greater than from eating poultry or pork.

- Each year, fish and chip shops sell some 60,000 tonnes of fish, most of it caught from around our coasts. Cod is the most popular. Cods are big, beautiful fish that come coloured anything from pale green to gold to red. When the male courts a female he does so with an elaborate display that includes swaying to and fro, grunting and croaking. A cod can live for up to twenty-five years, though few of them do.

- Pesticides, oil, heavy metals and sewage are dumped into the seas from which cod, plaice and haddock are taken. It is estimated there are some 100,000 manufactured chemicals polluting the North Sea, and the discharge from Sellafield makes the Irish Sea the most radioactive marine environment in the world.

- A Dutch investigation showed that 40 per cent of locally caught fish samples had bacterial skin diseases or cancerous tumours, and recommended an immediate reduction in the consumption of fish. Greenpeace suggested the level was closer to 50 per cent.

- As our seas become dirtier, fish farms become more widespread. These use such dubious practices as intense overcrowding, hormone injections, and the use of pesticides which may disperse into coastal waters; an increasing occurrence of blindness among wild salmon in sea lochs in the west of Scotland – an area with over 300 salmon farms – is almost certainly related to the use of the pesticide Nuvan 500 on farmed salmon.

- Some 4 or 5 million anglers spend millions of pounds each year on equipment to aid them in the torture and slaughter of fishes. Coarse fishing is the most popular; fish are caught with barbed hooks, dragged from their natural environment, then thrown into a crowded, suffocating keepnet. The 1911 Protection of Animals Act says that it is an offence to cause unnecessary suffering to domesticated and captive animals, which includes fishes. To deliberately hook and then drop a goldfish back into a bowl would be a criminal act; doing it to wild fishes is called a 'harmless hobby'.

● Because fishes don't show their pain in the same ways that mammals do, few people recognise fishing as the tragic carnage it is. Yet fish use their tongues and lips like hands – to gather food and build nests – making sport fishing both debilitating and cruel. Fishes who are caught but thrown back become vulnerable to infection and predation. Others are either battered to death or left to suffocate.

   Consider the following:

● 'Fish are very much "animals" with well-developed brains and nervous systems and are as likely to feel pain as any other vertebrate' (Patty Mark, Animal Liberation, Melbourne, Australia).

● A report published by Dutch scientists in 1988 gives evidence that fish experience pain and fear to a degree comparable to human reactions of the kind. Measuring the amount of pain and fear experienced by fish hooked during angling, the scientists ascertained that 'fish do experience fear and pain' (*Animals International*, 27 August 1988).

● Professor Frank Hird, eminent microbiologist of Melbourne University, Australia, has said, 'The suffering that arises from neglecting biological justice in the fishing industry appalls me in the extreme' (on the 1974 ABC science programme 'Insight'), and, 'It is unthinkable for me that animals do not have pain receptors. They need them in order to learn to survive dangerous situations. The argument which says that vertebrates such as fish do not feel pain is an argument of convenience' (April 1985).

● Hooking is extremely painful to fish, as they have rich innervation in their lips, tongue, and mouth. 'Playing' fish with a low-weight line causes fish great pain and stress, and veterinarians and scientists, as well as animal activists, have condemned the practice.

● Fishes can be remarkably compassionate. A South African publication documented a case of a deformed Black Moor goldfish called 'Blackie' and a Red Randi called 'Big Red' who saved his life. Blackie had trouble swimming and for over a year Big Red came to his rescue daily. The publication stated: 'Big Red constantly watches over his sick buddy, gently picking him up on his broad back and swimming him around the tank. When feeding-time approaches and their keeper sprinkles goldfish food on the surface, Big Red immediately picks up Blackie and swims him to the surface, where both feed.'

- An Australian government survey found that the two most highly regarded aspects of recreational fishing were to relax and unwind – 43 per cent; and to be outdoors – 28 per cent. Further down on the list was fishing for food – 7 per cent (Patty Mark, Animal Liberation).

SOLUTIONS

- Eat sea *vegetables* (seaweeds) instead of sea *animals*. Most wholefood and healthfood shops will offer at least one or two, if not a range to choose from. Use *nori* as a wrap for avocado and cucumber *sushi* (contrary to popular myth, *sushi* does not mean 'raw fish'!); try *wakame* or *kombu* in soups; or toast *nori* as a great salty snack. In restaurants, order pizza with mushrooms and green peppers, not anchovies; or have a veggie burger rather than a fish sandwich. Eating vegetables, legumes and fruits is the most compassionate thing you can do for fishes.
- Check department stores and pet shops in your area for unclean tanks, fishes floating on top, and signs of crowding; an inch-long tropical fish requires at least 12 square inches of water surface to breathe comfortably; a 2-inch fish needs twice as much. Complain (politely) to management if you find problems, and put your complaint in writing to the store owners and local press. Refuse to patronise their stores until the problems are eliminated, preferably with the discontinuation of fish sales altogether.
- Avoid visiting aquariums – either at home or abroad – which are nothing short of prisons for fishes and marine mammals. Encourage your family and friends to do the same.

RESOURCES

- Read *So you want to go fishing?* by Len Baker and Rina Milson

'(from Swan Song, P.O. Box 3, Beccles, Suffolk NR34 0DF; price £3). Not just about fishes but swans too.
- Campaign for the Abolition of Angling, P.O. Box 130, Sevenoaks, Kent TN14 5NR.

19

FOR THE BIRDS: HELPING OUR FEATHERED FRIENDS

A Robin Red breast in a Cage
Puts all Heaven in a Rage.

WILLIAM BLAKE, 'Auguries of Innocence'

So much for the idea that our feathered friends are all just bird brains.

DAVID STIPPS, staff reporter of the Wall Street Journal, from 'Einstein Bird Has Scientists Atwitter over Mental Feats' (profiling Alex, an African grey parrot who can name eighty of his favourite things, such as wool, walnut and shower, and 'can handle some simple abstractions as well as chimps and porpoises can')

The bird-catcher's trade and the bird-catcher's shop are alike full of horrors, and they are horrors which are due entirely to a silly fashion and a habit of callous thoughtlessness, not on the part of the ruffianly bird-catcher . . . who has to bear the burden of the odium attaching to these cruelties, but of the respectable customers who buy captured larks and linnets without the smallest scruple or consideration.

HENRY S. SALT, *Animals' Rights*

Incredible fact: By law, canaries are still kept at every coalmine in Britain. Each time a rescue team goes underground in an emergency, a canary must go with them.

THE PROBLEM

Who has not marvelled at the grace and beauty of birds, and wished for wings? In cities, suburbs, and rural areas, on the oceans and mountains, and even in the desert, the omnipresence of birds of myriad species, colours, sizes, and shapes is a reminder of the diversity of life. The coos of city pigeons, the unearthly hoots of owls, and the warbles of thrushes are so much a part of the fabric of our ecosystem that birds seem indomitable; but in fact birds are highly vulnerable beings who need protection. Consider just a few of the many ways in which birds are endangered by human encroachment and abuse:

- *Pesticides and other chemicals*: DDT killed millions of birds before its use was stopped in the early 1970s. Bald eagles, whose eggshells DDT made too fragile, are only now returning from the brink of extinction. Granular carbofuran, a pesticide used since 1969 on corn and other crops (despite an EPA report concluding that a single granule can kill a bird) is blamed for the deaths of 2 million eagles, hawks, shrikes, sparrows, finches, and other birds each year. Pigeons, often considered a nuisance, are sometimes deliberately poisoned. Again, no pesticide is safe for birds: even those designed for home use poison birds' water and food supplies.
- *Habitat destruction*: The single greatest threat to birds all over the world. Cities and suburbs expand, and dams and reactors are built, destroying forests and waterways that birds need in order to survive. In the Pacific Northwest of the USA, 1,200 acres of ancient forest, critical to owls and eagles, are felled each week for timber. Fifty-three acres of South American rainforest – the winter home to hundreds of species of songbirds, and year-round home to hundreds more – are felled each minute, many of them to create cheap cattle grazing land, primarily to satisfy the North American demand for fast-food burgers. Closer to home, the Somerset Levels are drying out. These, some of the last wet meadows in Britain, have long been a winter home to lapwings, golden plovers, Berwick's swans, and a perfect breeding ground for snipe, curlews and redshanks. Despite efforts to halt drainage by farmers, wildlife in the area continues to decline rapidly.
- *'Sport' and entertainment*: There are over 500 species of birds in Britain, most of whom can legally be shot either at any time, or during 'open' season. As a result, hunters maim and kill millions of wild ducks, geese, snipe, woodcocks, collared doves, pigeons and other species each year. Other birds specially bred so someone can have the pleasure of shooting

them down out of the sky include pheasants, partridges and quail. Pigeon-racers recently declared 'war' on a rare peregrine falcon and her young whom they suspected of attacking their pigeons; though plans to fit explosive devices on decoy pigeons caused an outcry and were dropped, shortly afterwards the falcon chicks were found battered to death.

- *Egg-collecting*: Rare and officially protected birds are under a different kind of threat. Collectors are now going to almost any lengths to obtain their eggs which, of course, are becoming increasingly valuable as extinction threatens. Though wardens and enthusiasts organise teams to guard nests from a distance, thieves are frequently successful. This is a criminal act for which those found guilty may have to pay large fines; unfortunately for the birds, this is not enough of a deterrent.

- *The exotic bird trade*: A quarter of a million or more parrots, macaws, cockatoos, fragile hummingbirds, and other 'exotic' birds are smuggled into affluent Western countries to be sold to pet shops and dealers, who in turn sell them at premium prices. These intelligent birds, many of whom pair for life and who can live sixty to eighty years or longer, are stuffed into false-bottom suitcases, sewn into the linings of coats, and jammed into pipes, hair rollers, or gutted auto parts, their beaks taped shut. The shockingly high mortality rate from this treatment only increases their rarity and, hence, their selling price.

WHAT YOU CAN DO TO HELP BIRDS

- Plant trees for nesting and bushes and other plants attractive to birds to help compensate for widespread destruction of their habitats. Shrubs that have berries – such as berberis, cotoneaster, holly and blackberries – can be valuable sources of food, especially in winter. Nest boxes and feeding tables will also encourage birds to settle (and, as an added benefit to both you and them, eat the insects attacking your plants).
    Caution: poinsettia and mistletoe are poisonous to birds!

- Install a birdbath with a coil heater in your garden, as well as a bird feeder. Remember to refill them both regularly, especially in winter, as birds' lives may depend on them. (Do not, however, put out nuts for birds during the spring and summer as the young can choke on them.)

- Cap your chimney; this simple step can save the lives of birds (and squirrels) who might otherwise fall in.

- Birds sometimes fly into windows and can be stunned, knocked out or, worst still, injured. They may do this because they see their own reflections and mistake them for 'intruders', or because they are attracted to something inside, or because the sky is reflected in the window. To prevent this, place diving hawk silhouettes, wind chimers, or streamers in the window, and close curtains or blinds whenever possible.

- If a bird enters your house the best way to help is to wait until dark, then open a window and put a light outside it. Turn out all house lights, and the bird should fly out to the light. If it is too long to wait for dark, try opening all the windows and doors anyway, and leave the bird alone. Your attempts to catch or encourage him or her towards the window are more likely to cause panic which may in turn result in injuries.

- *Never, never, never* buy a caged bird. Birds are flock animals, not loners, who need room to fly. Wild birds make sad, lonely, and sometimes dangerous 'pets'. Captive-bred birds are more docile, but breeders must constantly introduce new genes ('new blood') from wild-caught birds, so even buying only captive-bred birds supports the wild-caught bird trade.

- Discourage 'pet' shops from carrying birds. Tell friends, neighbours, and anyone who will listen just what happens to the birds who don't even make it to the shop. Complain to the managers of hotels and restaurants that keep caged birds.

- Never use poison or sticky substances to control pigeons, starlings, or other birds. If your city or town council does so, urge them to substitute humane forms of control.

- At weddings, throw bird seed or specially produced edible confetti instead of rice (which can swell in birds' stomachs, proving fatal to them).

- Remove kite string from trees – birds can get tangled up in it and die.

- Don't buy hats or anything else with feathers; birds may have been killed for their plumage. Also avoid down, which is often plucked from live geese.

RESOURCES

- Royal Society for the Protection of Birds (RSPB), The Lodge, Sandy, Bedfordshire, SG19 2D1, has a wide selection of books on every aspect of bird life, including how to care for those who visit your garden. They also have videos you can buy, and organise film shows around the country (open to the general public). Contact them for details.

20

BE A MOBILE ACTIVIST

Nothing is more powerful than an individual acting out of his conscience, thus helping to bring the collective conscience to life.

NORMAN COUSINS, *Human Options*

THE PROBLEM

The motto of the activist should be that of the Scout: *Semper Paratus* ('Be prepared'). Too often, we leave a situation saying, 'If only I had . . .'

Movements for social change thrive on visibility, but usually can't afford large advertising budgets. So, the 'Army of the Kind' must outfit itself with pamphlets and paraphernalia designed to turn heads and change minds. You'll find it helpful to stock up your cars, pockets, and backpacks with materials designed to raise people's consciousness.

THE SOLUTION

- If you have a car, use it to send a message to thousands of

21

IT'S RAINING CATS AND DOGS

People who let their dogs and cats have litters in order
to show their children the 'miracle of birth' should
come witness the 'miracle of death' performed in the
back rooms of animal shelters all over the country.

PHYLLIS WRIGHT, director of sheltering,
Humane Society of the United States

THE PROBLEM . . .

The British, they say, are a nation of animal lovers. And with an
estimated 12 million cats and dogs in the country, and one out of
every two homes having a 'pet', you would think this is true.
Yet the RSPCA reports that cruelty to animals is on the
increase, reported cases up 20% last year, dogs being the most
frequent victims (German shepherds coming top of the table),
but cats also being made to suffer for no reason other than that
they are there and vulnerable.

Millions of unwanted animals are dumped at dogs' homes or
abandoned in woods and on city streets, where they suffer not
just from hunger and lack of shelter, but often from street
violence, too. Many die slow and dreadful deaths. Luckier ones
are 'put to sleep' with an injection; the RSPCA euthanises a
staggering 1,000 dogs daily because their owners cannot be
found and no one else wants them. Even those who are re-
homed may (understandably) become 'difficult', their new
owners giving up, so that they are shunted through a series of
homes and heartbreaks: how do you explain to a dog why her
family abandoned her?

Unwanted cats and kittens are stuffed into polythene bags,
thrown into rivers and ponds and out of cars on motorways.

Yet still the population continues to grow, some animals
mated on purpose just for the pleasure of having baby animals

around, others allowed – or even encouraged – to roam unsupervised, to live 'natural' lives.

... Is Overwhelming

- A female dog reaches sexual maturity at about six months of age and comes into heat twice a year thereafter. She may give birth to a litter of puppies every six months. Female cats can be even more prolific, reaching sexual maturity at about the same age as dogs, but coming into heat every two to three weeks from February until late summer. One female cat may have three or four litters a year, with as many as six kittens per litter.

- Just one female cat and her offspring can produce forty-eight more cats in just sixteen months; and one female dog and her offspring can be responsible for the birth of 4,372 dogs in seven years!

- There is no way homes can be found for so many cats and dogs. Being humanely destroyed is probably one of the better things that can happen to them. Alternatives for cats include being used as bait with which to train hunting dogs or as tools in vivisection laboratories. Mongrel dogs and certain breeds are also popular with vivisectionists; stronger dogs may end up being torn apart in one of the illegal dog fights that are now becoming widespread.

THE SOLUTION

- Neuter and spay! Many societies now run low-cost spay/neuter programmes. Even paying the full cost for this once-in-a-lifetime operation beats the expense and trouble of dealing with unwanted litters.

- If your local shelter doesn't have such a programme, see if you can get one set up. In San Mateo County, California, USA, the number of animals handled by the Peninsula Humane Society dropped by 39 per cent from 1973 to 1974 when the county did just that. With overpopulation remaining a problem, San Mateo County recently implemented a moratorium on breeding companion animals, with violations punishable by a $100 fine!

- Never patronise 'pet' shops and breeders – they contribute to dog and cat overpopulation. The animals at your local shelter have personality, charm, and looks. *You* could be their lifeline.

What's the Procedure for Spaying and Neutering?

• Spaying or neutering is surgical sterilisation. Spaying of females involves the removal of the uterus and the ovaries, and usually requires an overnight stay at the vet's surgery. Neutering of males is done by removing the testicles, and dogs and cats can usually go home the same day. Many animal shelters (including the RSPCA) pre-sterilise adopted animals or require those who adopt animals to spay or neuter them. Spaying and neutering makes animals much less likely to roam in search of a breeding partner, or to fight for one. It also helps prevent mammary and testicular cancers. Altered males don't climb over or dig under fences to pursue females on heat across town and they don't spray furniture or curtains.

RESOURCES

• RSPCA, The Causeway, Horsham, West Sussex RH12 1HG; tel. (0403) 64181. Any animals re-homed by the society will have first been neutered, half the cost being paid by the society, the remainder by the new owner.

• Cats Protection League, 17 King's Road, Horsham, West Sussex RH13 5PP; tel. (0403) 65566. Has 200 branches distributed in all corners of the British Isles. Operates a Neutering Voucher Scheme to help those in need with the cost of neutering/spaying their cats. The amount varies with individual cases, though the owner is always required to pay part of the cost.

• National Canine Defence League, 1 Pratt Mews, London NW1 0AD; tel. (071) 388 0137. Most females are spayed before going to a new home, and in certain instances males are neutered.

• People's Dispensary for Sick Animals (PDSA), Whitechapel Way, Priorslee, Telford, Shropshire TF2 9PQ; tel. (0952) 290999. Principally there to help with sick and injured animals. If, however, you have a tom cat who is getting into

fights or wandering, they might be able to help. Talk to the vet at your nearest branch.
- The Cat Action Trust (CAT) PO Box 1639, London W8 4RY: an organisation caring specifically for feral cats. Spaying and neutering is a major aspect of their work. Contact the central office for details of your local group.

22

THANKS, BUT NO TANKS

I wish to tell you what we have learned of a group of uninhibited nudists who have never worn clothes... They have big brains and bright minds ...
DR JOHN LILLY, noted dolphin researcher,
in one of his many lectures on dolphins

Perhaps in some way I owe my medals to the dolphins. In their trusting and playful way, they taught me the subtleties of swimming technique.
MATT BIONDI, Olympic gold medal winner,
appealing to the US Congress to
strengthen the Marine Mammal Protection Act

THE PROBLEM

Dolphins: graceful, enigmatic, and revered – and the object of endless controversy. When the two companies which together have well over 50 per cent of the British market for tuna (John West and Princes) announced an end to their purchase of tuna from fishing companies that use seine nets (which, since the early 1960s, have killed over a quarter of a million dolphins annually), environmentalists and animal rights groups celebrated. However, because official observers on tuna fishing vessels are human, and therefore neither infallible nor able to be everywhere at once, and because the tuna suffer as well, a continuing boycott of tuna products can still help many animals, including the dolphins.

- In the 1960s there were thirty dolphinaria in Britain. Public outcry against the suffering they cause to dolphins and whales has meant that gradually more and more have closed until there are now just a couple. Two of the most recent to give up were Brighton Dolphinarium (notorious for its conditions, lack of daylight, and record of dolphin deaths, though the fate of the two surviving dolphins hasn't yet been decided) and Morecambe. Britain's one remaining captive killer whale, a female called Winnie, is still at Windsor Safari Park, although she is just about to be shipped to America where – although she won't be free – she will be able to live a better life with others of her own kind.
- There are, however, still dolphins at Flamingoland and Windsor Safari Park, plus disturbing reports of plans for more to be built in other parts of the country. Ric O'Barry trained the dolphin, Flipper, for the television show that captured the hearts of millions of American children. Flipper was, in fact, five different dolphins. It was when the one he used most often committed suicide in his arms (dolphins breathe by conscious effort and so can stop living whenever they choose) that he became an animal rights advocate. The dolphin was just a youngster. According to O'Barry, 'the average age of death of a captive dolphin is 5.8 years'. The average natural lifespan of free-roaming dolphins is twenty-five years.
- Although profiteers' publicists contend that dolphin and whale shows at dolphinaria teach viewers about animals, the overriding image is one of frivolity and artificiality, teaching nothing about the natural dignity and behaviour of these intelligent individuals or the plight of animals whose home is being polluted by human industry.
- In the USA, dolphins are being used in warfare. Former US Navy dolphin trainers like Rick Trout are speaking out publicly against the military conscription of these intelligent

and peace-loving mammals into involuntary service, where they are trained in manoeuvres hazardous to themselves and to humans. Forced to hunt mines, retrieve spent torpedoes, and 'de-activate' potential human saboteurs of barges and nuclear submarines, dolphins have become the military's favourite disposable soldiers. The Navy has used dolphins, sea lions and beluga whales in classified programmes since the 1960s and is now placing .45 calibre guns on the dolphins' snouts and training them to ram the devices, which trigger on impact, into 'enemy frogmen'. In 1988, the Seattle *Post-Intelligencer* reported that thirteen dolphins in training for the Navy's marine mammal programme had died during a two-year period; according to the report, nearly half of them suffered from depression, loss of appetite, stomach ulcers and severe stress before their deaths. (There are small victories: in January 1991, the US Navy declared a moratorium on the Pugent Sound, Washington, marine mammal programme.)

• Despite worldwide efforts to stop the use of seine nets to catch tuna (dolphins are just some of the many other-than-humans who get tangled up and die in these indiscriminate walls of death), they are still in common use.

Dolphin Documentation

• In the ocean, dolphins, who weigh 20-30 store, typically travel forty miles a day at speeds up to thirty-five miles per hour. It is frightening to contemplate what confinement does to mammals who navigate by sonar.

• At the National Aquarium in Baltimore, USA, dolphins spend 98 per cent of their time in the parts of their tanks furthest from spectators. Three bottlenose dolphins there developed ulcers in response to their inability to escape the crowds of people gathering to look at them, and one died.

• Because it is difficult to breed from captive dolphins, many of those who appear in dolphinaria around the world will have been captured in the wild. The first major task is to train the new arrival to overcome a natural desire to dive deep, and to spend most of her or his time instead in the 'open air' environment of the stage. Then the dolphin must be taught to do tricks. Trainers admit that this is achieved by restricting food to such an extent that the dolphin does whatever she or he is instructed to do in order to be fed. An especially gregarious dolphin might be punished for not performing as well as expected by being locked away from the other dolphins.

- The abuses dolphins have suffered at the hands of humans haven't stopped them from helping their awkward fellow earth-dwellers. In January of 1988, dolphins guided three ship-wrecked sailors to shore through shark-infested, turbulent waters a mile off South Africa's east coast. The dolphins reportedly stayed with the men throughout the full two-hour ordeal. Jacques Cousteau has documented a relationship between the people of Mauritania and dolphins, in which dolphins brought people fish.

- When the Dalai Lama won the Nobel Peace Prize in 1989, eighteen Tibetan monks celebrated by chanting to dolphins at the Miami Seaquarium. Marine scientists said the sound waves produced by the chanting were pleasing to the dolphins, who kept their heads out of the water, some tilting their heads to the side to hear better.

THE SOLUTION

- Never go to dolphinaria or other places advertising performing dolphins or whales. If you want to see these beautiful creatures in their natural environment, buy or hire a video.

- Now and again a dolphin arrives in a bay on the British coast, and decides – of his/her own will – to stay around for a few weeks, or even longer. Dolphin enthusiasts have been known to swim with these truly wild dolphins, and say it is the experience of a lifetime. If you'd like to know more about these and other dolphins, and why we need to preserve their environment, join the Dolphin Circle (8 Dolby Road, London SW6 3NE) and receive their informative quarterly magazine.

- If there is a dolphinarium near you – or you hear of plans to open one – resolve to stop it. Write to your local newspaper and your MP stating your objections. Suggest a display of animal models, aquatic plants and coral reefs instead. Go to see the Cousteau Oceanic Park in Paris, which exhibits models of sea creatures enhanced by special effects and audio-visual processes to create an underwater environment. Other attractions include a theatre programme that simulates an ocean descent and a walk-in model of a pregnant blue whale.

- Join the growing number of societies and individuals calling for a complete ban on the use of seine nets. Inform friends, family and work colleagues about these 'walls of death' and the millions of birds and animals they kill each year, including dolphins.

RESOURCES

- Whale and Dolphin Conservation Society, 19a James Street West, Bath BA1 2BT.
- Sea Shepherd UK, P.O. Box 5, Ashford, Middlesex TW15 2PY. (Also try to get hold of *Sea Shepherd: My Fight for Whales and Seals* by Paul Watson. Inspiring. Makes you want to get out there and save the seas!)
- International Dolphin Watch, Parklands, North Ferriby, Humberside HU14 3ET. Trying to save dolphins by promoting the way in which they not only relate to human beings, but can actually help people suffering from depression. Has produced a moving fifty-minute film called *Bewitched by a Dolphin*, which helps prove the point (price £14.95 plus £1.05 p&p). Send for it to show at home or at a fund-raising evening; or – better still – get your local TV station to transmit it.
- Captive Animals' Protection Society, 36 Braemore Court, Kingsway, Hove, East Sussex BN3 4FG. Campaigns on behalf of all captive performing animals, including those in dolphinaria.

23

FUR IS DEAD

Fur used to turn heads, now it turns stomachs.
RUE McCLANAHAN

THE PROBLEM
The good news is, the fur industry feels trapped. Since vigorous anti-fur campaigns have begun, fur trade journals report that the 'harvest' of wild animals for fur has dropped as much as 80 per cent. Harrods announced in March 1990 that its fur salon would close; other well-established fur shops have recently done the same, including Sacks and Brendler in Chelmsford (after forty years), and Faulkes Fur, which started business in Birmingham over sixty years ago. Leaders in the fashion industry, including Giorgio Armani, Bill Blass, and Norma Kamali, have pledged never again to work with fur.

The bad news is, every year approximately 44 million animals are still killed for the production of fur. Though Britain is one of the seventy countries that have banned leg-hold traps, much of the fur we import has been obtained this way. For every 'target' animal trapped, three 'trash' animals (e.g., cats, dogs, deer, and birds) are killed. One 40-inch-long wild mink coat can represent sixty 'target' animals and 180 unintended victims. So for each fur bought, up to 240 animals can lose their lives, needlessly suffering a combined total of up to 3,600 hours in traps. That's more than five months of agony per coat.

Trapping Truths
• Most fur garments (about 74 per cent) are derived from animals killed by trappers, a large percentage of them coming from North America and Canada. It has been estimated that, every year, some 24 million coyotes, foxes, raccoons, lynxes, rabbits, bobcats, muskrats, sables, opossums and other animals find themselves locked in the spring-loaded,

steel-jawed leg-hold traps that so many countries have now banned (some US states also ban their use – including Florida, Rhode Island and New Jersey).

- The shock suffered by animals when caught in a leg-hold trap is, as behaviourist Dr Desmond Morris has explained, 'difficult for us to conceive, because it is a shock of total lack of understanding of what has happened to them. They are held, they cannot escape, their response very often is to bite at the metal with their teeth, break their teeth in the process and sometimes even chew through the leg that is being held in the trap.' Up to one in four trapped animals (around 2 million per year) chews off his or her own leg or foot to escape, but those who drag themselves away from the traps often die later of blood loss, predation (because they are no longer quick enough to escape), or infection. Trapped animals who do not die before the trapper arrives (often days later) are shot, beaten, or stamped to death; trappers are taught to stand on the animal's chest and yank the hind legs out, crushing the lungs.

- The number of animals needed to make a 40-inch coat varies, depending on the animal used: fifteen beavers, sixteen coyotes, eighteen lynxes, forty-five opossums, fifty muskrats. (Multiply by three to get the total number of animals killed per coat.)

- Trapping is not an effective tool for 'wildlife management', contrary to fur-industry propaganda. Trapping disrupts wildlife populations by killing healthy animals needed to keep the species strong, and populations are further damaged when the parents of young animals are killed.

Fur Factory Farms

- Though the demand for fur in Britain has diminished, there are still some fifty farms producing mink in the country, and at least three farms breeding foxes. Their lives are much like those of other factory farmed animals, except that, being undomesticated animals, they may suffer even more.

- Animals on fur farms live their short lives in wire mesh cages, victims of stress, fear, and self-mutilation. In the interests of profit, animals are dispatched by the cheapest methods possible, which are usually also the most crude and cruel, e.g., anal electrocution, poisoning with weed killer, and suffocation.

- Foxes are kept in wire mesh cages so small that they can only take a few steps in any direction. The floors too are made of large-gauge wire so that the pads of the paws poke through, becoming cut and sore. Some foxes pace restlessly, others press themselves nervously into a corner. Many die of diseases that are rife under such conditions.

- Though fox farmers insist their animals are of domestic origin, the arctic fox is being bred by at least one farmer in this country to supply the demand for white fur at home and also abroad (many pelts go to Finland). Unlike the British fox, who has a somewhat limited territory, wild arctic foxes will roam over vast areas every day.

- Mink are wild creatures who have been bred in captivity only a short time. They are also solitary animals who, under natural circumstances, try to avoid each other. On farms, however, they may be in a unit containing many thousands of animals and are generally kept in very small cages, probably having to share with one or more other animals, despite the fact that overcrowding of this kind results in a 1 per cent loss of animals due to fighting and cannibalism. Bred to be larger and have thicker fur than wild minks, they are especially vulnerable to heat; in 1987, US mink farmers reported that 450,000 animals died of heat stress on their farms.

- Other animals too are factory farmed for their fur; rabbits in particular are slaughtered in their millions to make 'coney' fur jackets.

- South Korea has become one of the leading fur manufacturing countries of the world. In 1987, its exports to the US, Europe, and Japan amounted to $115 million, and they continue to rise.

THE SOLUTION

- *Don't wear fur*, and avoid toys (such as real mink teddies!) and other items made with fur. If you are attached to the fur 'look', or know someone who is, give yourself or your friend a fake. '*Faux* fur' has become a fashion statement among many designers who are opposed to the cruelty real fur represents.

- If you already have a fur, send it to Lynx, who will add it to the many furs that have been handed over by women and men who no longer wish to be seen supporting such cruelty. Eventually the furs are to be destroyed in a public ceremony.
- Don't shop in department stores with fur boutiques, or in stores that carry fur clothing, accessories, or toys. Write or speak to the store managers to let them know you oppose the inhumane treatment of animals. Don't buy secondhand furs either. (In 1990 Oxfam announced it would no longer accept donations of furs for sale in its shops.)
- A number of magazines regularly promote furs. If you spot a feature that offends you, write at once to the editor (the address will be in the front of the magazine) saying that you are disappointed that they feel the need to promote cruelty to animals. Point out that a number of surveys have been carried out recently, all of them indicating that the majority of people (more than seven out of ten) think it wrong to kill animals for their fur. What's more, in a Gallup survey 85 per cent of those who took part stated that they consider real fur coats to be out of fashion!
- Newspapers, too, can be persuaded to adopt a fur-free policy. The national newspaper *Today* has already agreed to do so, the editor David Montgomery tellying Lynx: 'knowing of *Today*'s views fur advertisers would be mad to ever approach us in the future'.
- Support anti-fur legislation. A number of groups (including Lynx, Beauty Without Cruelty and the Animal Protection Foundation) are campaigning to change attitudes and the law in this country. Working to ban the import of fur caught by leg-hold traps (or at least gaining the assurance that all furs caught this way would be so labelled) is one approach being taken; completely phasing out fur factory farms is another.
- Join rallies and demonstrations to help teach others that trapping and fur farming are destructive practices stemming from greed, not glamour.

RESOURCES

- Lynx (P.O. Box 300, Nottingham NG1 5HN) was formed specifically to fight the fur industry. They do this on many different fronts, including widespread advertising to encourage the public to see fur for what it really is. Write for details of their work and latest campaign.
- Though Beauty Without Cruelty is a society that tackles various problems relating to the fashion and beauty aspect of animal abuse, fur is a key issue on their agenda. Contact them at 57 King Henry's Walk, London N1 4NH.
- Animal Protection Foundation (P.O. Box 168, Cardiff, CF5 5YH) are very much involved with the fight to close British fur farms and are currently working to put one of the last arctic fox farms out of business. In order to focus media attention on what life is really like in these places, they organise peaceful demonstrations and invite the Press along. Why not join them?

24

STOP PICKING ON PIGS

I have a friendly feeling towards pigs generally, and consider them the most intelligent of beasts . . . I also like his attitudes towards all other creatures, especially man . . . He views us from a totally different, a sort of democratic standpoint as fellow citizens and brothers, and takes for granted, or grunted, that we understand his language, and without servility or insolence he has a natural, pleasant, camerados-all or hail-fellow-well-met air with us.

Naturalist W.H. HUDSON, *Book of a Naturalist*
(as quoted in John Robbins' *Diet for A New America)*

THE PROBLEM

Pigs are among the least understood and most persecuted of all animals. They are personable and clean (if allowed room to escape their own waste), and their intelligence exceeds that of our close companion, the dog. Yet pigs spend their much-shortened lives in bleak factory buildings, suffering abuses that would create a national outcry if inflicted on 'man's best friend'. Fifteen million pigs are slaughtered annually for British dinnertime fare like pork chops. Far away from a mud wallow or the sounds and smells of the forests and jungles which were once their homes, virtually all the pigs raised for pork, bacon, and sausages are produced under intensive farming methods, housed in cramped unsanitary conditions, barely able to move.

● *Breeders*: 'The breeding sow should be thought of, and treated, as a valuable piece of machinery whose function is to pump out baby pigs like a sausage machine' (I.J. Taylor, Export Development Manager, Wall's Meat Company).

'Farrowing operations' is the industry term for breeding factories, whose aim is to churn out as many pigs per litter and as many litters per year as possible. There are about

800,000 breeding sows who are either fertilised by boars (on what farmers call 'rape racks'), or artificially inseminated. Farmers often use large doses of hormones to ensure constant fertility. Once pregnant, over half of these sows are kept in dry-sow stalls, usually tethered by the waist or neck, standing on concrete and metal grating, unable to turn or move for almost four months until the piglets are born (ten is the usual number). The sow will be with them for just three weeks, confined this time in a tight metal crate so that she does not accidentally roll over and kill one. When she is parted from them she will fight and try to return to them, watched by her bewildered young. She will not, of course, win. About a week later she will again be 'serviced' by the boar or artificially inseminated. On average, sows survive five pregnancies before they are slaughtered.

- *Feeders*: 'Forget the pig is an animal. Treat him like a machine in a factory. Schedule treatments like you would lubrication. Breeding like the first step in an assembly line. And marketing like the delivery of finished goods' (J. Brynes, Hog Farm Management).

Most piglets are raised in flat deck cages packed in rooms that are kept swelteringly hot (despite a deficiency of sweat glands that means they have a poor heat regulating mechanism). First though they will have had their tails cut off to prevent neurotic tail-biting, behaviour that results from close confinement), their ears notched, their teeth clipped, and the males will have been castrated, all without anaesthetics. Sometime between eighteen and twenty-four weeks they will be dragged, kicked, and/or goaded with an electric prodder to the truck that will give them their first and last sight of daylight.

Still Fancy that Bacon Sandwich?

In 'Watching the Animals' (*Harper's*, March 1970), Richard Rhodes wrote of the last hours of pigs' lives: 'Before they reach their end, the pigs get a shower, a real one. Water sprays from every angle to wash the farm off them. Then they begin to feel crowded. The pen narrows like a funnel; the drivers behind urge the pigs forward, until one at a time they climb on to the moving ramp . . . Now they scream, never having been on such a ramp, smelling the smells they smell ahead . . . It was a frightening experience, seeing their fear, seeing so many of them go by, it had to remind me of things no one wants to be reminded of any more, all mobs, all death marches, all mass murders and executions.'

- 'Modern' pigs, bred for more meat, develop painful foot and leg lesions because they can't support their extra weight.
- Because of stress, some factory pigs 'freeze-up': they become so afraid that they cannot move, even to eat or drink. Others remain in constant panicked motion, a neurotic perversion of their instinct to escape.
- Approximately 30 per cent of all pork products are contaminated with toxoplasmosis, a disease caused by parasites that can be passed on to consumers. Salmonella poisoning is frequently traced back to pork. Recent surveys also revealed that at least one in twenty pigs contains residues of the antibacterial drug, sulphadimidine, grossly exceeding the ministry's permitted levels. (The drug is suspected by the US Food and Drug Administration of causing cancer.)
- A large number of pigs die before they are slaughtered. Most die from respiratory disease brought on by enclosed housing and aggravated by crowding and stress. Pneumonia is widespread, as is pleurisy, peritonitis and TB. Many more die en route to the slaughterhouse; prone to heart attacks, they find the overcrowded conditions, plus the sudden shock of being away from the pens in which they have lived their lives, just too much.

THE SOLUTION . . .
. . . is much less complex than the problem: don't eat pig flesh in any form, including ham, bacon, sausages, and hotdogs.

- Beware of pig by-products such as lard, which is sometimes used in commercial foods.
- Try an alternative; some are eerily close to the 'real thing'. Check at your local wholefood store for Protoveg's 'Sosmix' which can be made into sausages (and sausage rolls!), and

'Sizzles' Smokey Bacon Flavour shapes. Protoveg also do a pork-flavoured loaf. Granose Soya-Franks are an excellent substitute for hotdogs. Or make your own sausage mix from nuts and/or beans, breadcrumbs, herbs, plus soy sauce to get the distinctive salty taste. Look out too for 'bacon' bits, which are deliciously crunchy and are made from textured vegetable protein; good over soups or salads. Or try grilling very thin strips of *tempeh* until crisp, then crumble them and use in the same way. Serve barbecued *tofu* in a rich (vegetarian!) sauce.

- Encourage your local MP to support a Bill currently going through Parliament to phase out the inhumane practice of fettering sows and keeping them in close confinement. Suggest that this should be passed immediately (intensive farms want a ten-year phasing-out period).

25

BRINGING ANIMALS INTO THE FOLD

> There is no religion without love, and people may talk as much as they like about their religion, but if it does not teach them to be good and kind to other animals as well as humans, it is all a sham.
>
> ANNA SEWELL, author of *Black Beauty*

> Until he extends the circle of his compassion to all living things, Man will not himself find Peace.
>
> ALBERT SCHWEITZER

BACKGROUND

Religion, one of whose tenets traditionally has been reverence for life (including respect for animals and the earth), is one of the strongest and most influential institutions in our society, and is a guiding force for hundreds of millions of people. What an impact organised religion can have when it embraces concern for all animals; yet what is preached often may not be what is practised.

Virtually every religious tradition, from Christianity to Jainism, and from Hinduism to Judaism, extols the virtues of compassion and mercy. Many religious leaders and theologians, including Mohandas K. Gandhi, Dr Albert Schweitzer, and the Reverend Norman Vincent Peale, have fervently argued the rights of other-than-human beings and the importance of making the ethical treatment of all animals a theological priority. This is a powerful and significant heritage.

WHAT YOU CAN DO

- Make your church or synagogue a place of all-encompassing compassion. Worcester and Salisbury cathedrals are just two of the places where services are held to bless and pray for animals – persuade others to follow their excellent example.

- Watch and share the film *We Are All Noah*, a thirty-minute documentary on religious perspectives of animal welfare and rights, with family, friends, and religious groups. Available on loan from Quaker Concern for Animals' Welfare (contact their Literature Secretary, Roy Chadwick, 75 Laburnum Avenue, Wickford, Essex SS12 0DB.)
- To get a book list, prayer booklet, newsletter, and names and addresses of the fourteen British societies that come under the Christian Consultative Council for the Welfare of Animals, write to the CCCWA at 269 Belstead Road, Ipswich, Suffolk IP2 9DY.
- For a free booklet on religion, animals and nature protection, send a self-addressed envelope to the Interfaith Council for the Protection of Animals and Nature (ICPAN) (2841 Colony Road, Ann Arbor, MI 48104, USA), an organisation dedicated to persuading clergy, religious leaders, and laypeople of all faiths and denominations that their help is needed if we are going to stop the ecological destruction of our planet.
- Vegetarian seders are now held in cities around the world at Passover. Contact the International Jewish Vegetarian Society, 855 Finchley Road, London NW11 8LX, for a book list that includes recipes. According to Steven Rosen, author of the book *Food for the Spirit*, the first ten generations of Jews (from Adam to Noah) were frugivorous vegetarians.

RESOURCES

- *Animals and All Churches* is a thought-provoking little book by centenarian Victoria Lidiard (price £1.00 from M. Seelig, Unity Centre, Suite 4, Carlton Chambers, 5 Station Road, Shortlands, Bromley, Kent BR2 0EY).
- International Network for Religion and Animals (INRA), 2913 Woodstock Avenue, Silver Spring, MD 20910, USA. Objective: to bring religious principles to bear upon humanity's attitude towards the treatment of non-human animals. INRA is ecumenical and international in its scope.
- Jews for Animal Rights, 255 Humphrey Street, Marblehead, MA 01945, USA, provides education about animal abuse, and

influences Jewish communities to change attitudes and behaviour; illuminates role of Jewish people and their relationship to animals. Free literature, periodical newsletter, no membership dues.

- Unitarian Universalists for Ethical Treatment of Animals (UFETA), 230 W. 78th Street, New York, NY 10024, USA. UFETA works with over 1,000 congregations to introduce the issue of animal rights and to initiate observances on church calendars (Meat-Out Day, World Day for Animals in Laboratories, World Prayer Week for Animals, etc.); encourages congregations nationwide to adopt resolutions for the rights of animals and to incorporate the philosophy and language into sermons; sponsors a major animal rights speaker every June at the General Assembly to address the over 5,000 attendees who are mostly religious educators, ministers etc. (Membership for individuals or organisations. Contributors receive a newsletter twice a year in addition to several other mailings.)

26

HALT THE HUNT

You ask people why they have deer heads on the wall. They always say, 'Because it's such a beautiful animal.' There you go. I think my mother's attractive, but I have photographs of her.
ELLEN DEGENERES, 'On Location: Women of the Night'

The squirrel that you kill in jest, dies in earnest.
HENRY D. THOREAU, *Familiar Letters*

THE PROBLEM
For the first time since medieval times, blood sports are on the

increase. Some of these are illegal: badger-baiting, dog-fighting and cock-fighting were banned many years ago, and the new interest in these horrifying 'sports' is condemned by all except a minority. Just the same, it is estimated that some 9,000 badgers are killed by dogs each year. Few of the organisers of these unfair 'fights' are caught, and those who do end up in court usually get away with a fine (though legislation to make such crimes punishable with a term in prison may soon be accepted).

There are other blood sports, however, that are not only allowed, but actually have their own society; the British Field Sports Society. This is the hunters' protective body, formed to stand up for the rights of a group of grown men and women to terrify, torture and eventually kill defenceless and innocent animals for no other reason than that it amuses them to do so.

Hunters might well need a protective body. Surveys carried out over the last twenty years show that the public is increasingly disturbed about fox-, stag- and mink-hunting, and hare-coursing, with the 'anti's' growing in number daily. In 1987, a Gallup survey showed 73 per cent were in favour of a ban on stag-hunting, while 68 per cent wanted fox-hunting stopped. Yet the killing continues.

H(a)unting Facts
- The official fox-hunting season is from November until April. There are nearly 200 hunts in the country, each with an average pack of sixty dogs (bred for stamina *not* speed – or the chase would be over too quickly!), most of the hunts going out about fifty times during the season. Though some 7,500 foxes will be killed by the hunt each year, another 8,500 fox cubs will be used as bait during the hound training sessions. As the hunting season also coincides with the breeding season, many vixens will be killed whilst heavily pregnant, and newborn cubs will starve to death in their earth when their mothers fail to return.
- Hunters claim they are keeping down the fox population. In fact, the numbers they kill do not begin to compare with the numbers despatched by snares or road accidents. They claim it is an effective way to kill them; shooting by trained

marksmen would be quicker and much kinder. They say farmers think of the fox as a pest; but as foxes are efficient at controlling vermin, and only rarely go for lambs or chickens (some 95 per cent of chickens are bred well out of reach in factory farms, and research shows that few lambs are killed by foxes), the majority of farmers disagree. In fact, they're likely to suffer more damage and inconvenience from hunts crossing their land (hounds often attack sheep and may cause pregnant sheep to abort, causing more deaths than foxes do).

- A research project in 1983 showed that a total of £86m a year is spent on fox-hunting. That works out at £11,500 for each fox killed.

- Deer are hunted by four packs in the South of England. (In Scotland, where there is an annual deer cull, they are shot – a preferable death for the animal, providing the marksman is skilled.) A chosen stag is separated out, at first moving easily, not knowing that he is to provide a day's entertainment. After maybe a whole day of running, trying to find sanctuary but continually flushed out by supporters, his body growing exhausted, his step unsure, he will probably seek a final sanctuary in water. When eventually he is shot he may be twenty-five miles from where the hunt started. A hind may well be pregnant when she is forced to flee from the dogs, her pace slower, so that the dogs may be on her before a marksman can catch up; they will go for her stomach. If she has a calf running with her she will do all she can to encourage him to run on, but he will, of course, refuse to leave the 'safety' of her side.

- In 1990, public concern about the cruelty involved in hunting deer with dogs forced the National Trust to let its members vote on whether the hunt should be allowed on Trust property. When, however, the result was a firm 'no', the Trust decided to put off a decision about instigating a ban for a further two years.

- Don't think that the dogs get a good deal either. Most of those in hunt packs are shot before they reach five years of age; a dog must be young and fit to follow the prey. Mr Robin McKenzie, the Master of the Hampshire-based Vine and Craven fox-hunt said that 'On average, each hunt breeds thirty-six pups from six bitches each year and twelve of these pups are selected and entered into the pack.' The League Against Cruel Sports point out that this means twenty-four of these pups and twelve adult hounds are killed annually by the hunt. Dogs are also injured or killed during the hunt itself, especially those based close to urban areas where there are busy roads or railway lines to be crossed.

- Mink-hunting is the summer blood sport, filling the gap for the brief time when foxes and deer are protected. Though native to North America, mink were brought to this country for fur farms earlier this century. When the fur market collapsed many breeders simply released them into the wild. There are twenty-one mink-hunt packs, men following on foot as they search the river banks for the scent of a mink. After a short chase the terrified animal will try to seek sanctuary; the hunters may have to dig him/her out of holes in the bank, or drag the small struggling body down from a tree. Although there is no specific ban on otter-hunting as such, it is against the law to kill an otter, so mink-hunting has taken the place of this 'sport' (thousands of otters were killed in the late fifties and the sixties, bringing the animal close to extinction). The damage caused by packs hunting mink along river banks also poses a threat to the small remaining otter population.

- Hares, once a familiar sight, are now also declining in numbers dramatically. Unlike rabbits, they breed above ground, so the young are in danger of being killed by heavy machinery, pesticides and herbicides. To make matters worse, some 10,000 of them are killed each year as a result of beagling or coursing. Beagling is much like fox-hunting in that the supporters follow a pack of dogs, only this time they do so on foot, and the quarry is the hare. As with fox-hunting, the exhausted animal rarely escapes and will more likely be torn to pieces by the dogs. The aim of hare-coursing is for two dogs (often greyhounds) to compete against each other, spectators betting on the one they think will perform best. A wild hare is driven past the dogs who are then released to 'course' it, a mounted judge awarding points for each dog's ability to turn the hare. Eventually the hare becomes a living 'rope' in a tug of war; it may take several minutes before the handlers get close enough to reach the dogs and the hare may still be alive and screaming. Contrary to the eloquent claims of those who support these 'sports', the hare is not a pest; in many areas it is so rare it has to be introduced specially for coursing.

- Some 850,000 people are licensed to have guns in the UK. Of the 600,000 estimated to be regular users, only 3 per cent do not shoot live quarry.

THE SOLUTION

Hunted animals cannot defend themselves against an establishment that sees nothing wrong with killing animals for entertainment, so we must become active on their behalf. Here are ways to protect wildlife and thwart hunters:

- Join forces with the Hunt Saboteurs. This is an organisation made up of people dedicated to non-violent, direct action against blood sports. In other words, they do everything they can to confuse the hounds to give the hunted animal at least a chance to escape. This they do by imitating the huntsman's use of horn and his calls, spraying liquids to disguise the quarry's scent. If you'd sooner go it alone, get some tips from the HSA's *Tactics Book* (price £1 from their office).
- If hunters use dogs in your area, use Antimate spray, sprinkle a female dog's urine in heavily hunted areas, or spray a solution of chopped garlic cloves soaked in water or diluted lemon juice on leaves and trails to throw dogs off the scent.
- Go into the woods the day before the hunting season begins, and loudly play a radio or recordings of wolf howls, and walk with dogs on leads. Such tactics are particulary important for scattering younger animals who have not yet known the traumatising experience of being hunted.
- Encourage anti-hunt sentiments in your area by writing letters to the editors of local newspapers, talking to neighbours, and ringing local radio talk-ins. Try to tie in with some special event or happening such as the first day of the fox-hunting season, or the Boxing Day hunt (a highlight of the hunting fraternity's Christmas celebrations); take

action if a hunt has damaged local property, or killed someone's companion animals (as often happens).

- Educate yourself and others by reading and distributing books and literature that tell the truth about hunting. The League Against Cruel Sports provides the facts in an easy-to-read form. Get public and school libraries to add such reading to their lists; if necessary, donate copies yourself.
- Before you support a 'wildlife' or 'conservation' group, ask for its policy statement on hunting. The World Wide Fund for Nature do not oppose hunting; the Woodland Trust and the National Trust actually allow hunting on their land. Of course these societies also do a lot of good work on behalf of animals, and you needn't necessarily stop your contributions to them. Instead, you might let them know you'd be a lot happier if they would consider the rights of not just some but *all* animals.
- Distribute leaflets on hunting (available from many societies including the Hunt Saboteurs and the League Against Cruel Sports). Leave them in buses, doctors' waiting rooms; inside library books that you return.

RESOURCES
- Hunt Saboteurs Association (HSA), P.O. Box 1, Carlton PDO, Nottingham NG4 2JY.
- League Against Cruel Sports, 83–87 Union Street, London SE1 1SG.
- Well worth reading: *The Politics of Hunting* by Richard Thomas (Gower 1983).

27

GET POLITICAL

Ever occur to you why some of us can be this much concerned with animals suffering? Because government is not. Why not? Animals don't vote.

PAUL HARVEY

All progressive legislation has always had its genesis in the mind of one person. In the long run, it is the cumulative effect that matters. One can do much. And one and one can move mountains.

JOAN WARD-HARRIS, *Creature Comforts*

THE PROBLEM

Other-than-human beings do not have a Bill of Rights – and they certainly don't have representatives in Parliament. Elected officials usually respond to issues involving other-than-humans only when their human constituents compel them to. An essential part of any movement for social change is the effort to create new legislation, and since other-than-humans can't vote and can't lobby for themselves, we are responsible for making their concerns a political priority.

A Bit of Background

In the early 1820s, a Bill to protect animals was laughed out of Parliament, though it wasn't long afterwards that the Ill-Treatment of Cattle Act became Britain's first English statute prohibiting cruelty to animals. It was also about this time that the RSPCA was set up – not just to prosecute under the new laws, but to endeavour to change people's attitudes to animals in general. Laws that came into force in the 1830s helped make the lives of domestic animals and Hackney carriage horses somewhat better. Bull-baiting and cock-fighting were also outlawed, and in 1870 the last bullfight was held in Britain; the Spaniards who had organised the event were successfully prosecuted and fined.

Although the original Bill did slightly improve conditions in slaughterhouses, it wasn't until 1933 that it became compulsory to use the captive bolt pistol (designed to render animals unconscious before slaughter) on all animals except pigs. (A law enforcing the pre-stunning of pigs came into force in the 1950s.) A survey by the RSPCA recently revealed that over 6 per cent of animals stunned by the captive bolt pistol (which propels a bolt into the brain by compressed air or a blank cartridge) are less than fully stunned because of badly aimed shots or inadequately powered pistols. Some animals – chickens in particular – are stunned most often by an electric shock, though this method also fails to ensure that the animal feels no pain. 'Ritual' kosher and halal slaughter, an integral part of the Jewish and Moslem faiths, requires that animals be fully conscious when their throats are cut, and though there have been many campaigns to prevent this method of slaughter being carried out in Britain, so far it is still permitted by law.

There have been only two important laws passed regarding animals in experimental laboratories. The first was the 1876 Cruelty to Animals Act, brought in because of concern about the 'hideous, diabolic and horrendous' experiments being carried out by vivisectionists on some 300 animals each year. The 1986 Animals (Scientific Procedures) Act was brought in to help tighten laws regarding experiments that now totalled millions. Though public concern and improved alternatives have meant a gradual reduction in such experiments, many animal rights societies feel that the main achievement of these acts was not the prevention of animal suffering, but the legalisation of vivisectionists' work.

Ultimately it seems that, in law, animals still have no rights and no status. Legally classified as a commodity, they are – perhaps not surprisingly – treated as such.

WHAT YOU CAN DO

- Help political candidates who are sympathetic to animal issues get elected by joining their campaigns. In Parliament there are now a number of MPs committed to animal protective legislation. There is an All-Party Parliamentary Group for Animal Welfare which aims to keep animal issues to the fore. There is even a self-confessed vegetarian: Labour MP Tony Benn!

- Support any Bills introduced to help animals. There are many changes due in 1992 (with the creation of a 'Free market' for all European Community member states), so now is the time to campaign for all the legislation that is needed to ensure Britain maintains its reputation for caring about animals. Many of our hard-fought laws are in imminent danger of being wiped out overnight. Currently it isn't obligatory to test cosmetics on animals in Britain; after 1992 it might be. Our export in live horses has stopped completely over recent years; but after 1992 it may begin all over again. The conditions in our slaughterhouses – though horrifyingly medieval – are considerably better than those in continental slaughterhouses. Most of the societies involved with animals are now rallying support from members, asking them to write to their MPs and Euro MPs; also to campaign on a local level so that the general public are aware of what could happen, and to get those in agreement to sign petitions. Once most campaigning was about improving conditions for animals; at this time much of our concern must be directed towards maintaining them.

- Get acquainted with your local councillors; find out who they are by calling your council offices. Write to your local Member of Parliament (c/o The House of Commons, Westminster, London SW1A 0AA), bringing up any animal rights issues you feel are important on a local, national or international level. Keep your letter short (politicians are busy people) but make your point. In addition to holding open meetings in your area, your MP will also hold regular 'surgeries' at which he or she will discuss with you any issues you wish. If you feel a talk of this kind would be worthwhile, let your MP know that you will attend next time one is scheduled in your area. Consider taking along a like-minded supporter. Most local councillors and MPs are aware of the growing concern about animal abuse – even those whose political leanings you may not agree with could be powerful allies when it comes to, for example, your concern about the phasing out of dry-stalls for sows, or the hunting of deer on local property.

- When meeting an elected official personally:
    - ○ Make an appointment well in advance.
    - ○ Dress conservatively and professionally.
    - ○ Be prompt and patient.
    - ○ Be friendly and positive.
- Don't forget to:
    - ○ Do your homework ahead of time.
    - ○ Learn as much as you can about the person you are to meet – his or her political career to date, interests, soft spots!
    - ○ Compliment him or her on any political accomplishments you admire.
- Know your facts, provide one-page fact sheets and/or background information, make your points clearly and succinctly – and reasonably (dispel the stereotype that animal advocates are emotional saps). Always thank him or her for listening, and say you hope he or she will give your comments serious consideration.
- Think creatively. There are lots of things you can do to help put across your message more memorably. In the USA, Ohio members of Protect Our Earth's Treasures (POET) countered the National Pork Products Council's offer to Ohio legislators of a free ham-and-cheese lunch with that of a free, healthful, vegetarian sandwich lunch, which they delivered to legislators' offices along with information on the environmental and health consequences of eating meat.
- Write letters. When writing to an elected official, discuss only one issue in each letter, and keep it short (one page). Legibly handwritten letters are best – the more personal the letter appears, the more seriously it will be taken. Use personal or business stationery with a return address; and if you are a constituent, make that clear. Spell out all important details of the issue (don't assume the official knows anything about it), support your argument with facts, and state clearly and simply what you want her or him to do. Don't be vague.
- If you want to simply express your support for a proposed law regarding animals (one which requires no explanation), consider doing so on a postcard. This saves both you and your MP's office staff valuable time. Just write a few words to ask

your MP to add your name to the many you know are writing to him or her on a particular issue, adding that you are sure he or she will do everything possible to ensure the proposed Bill becomes law. (For experimentation issues you could buy cards ready printed with a short message, available from the Humane Research Trust, Brook House, 29 Bramhall Lane South, Bramhall, Cheshire SK7 2DN.)

- Consider standing as a local candidate yourself for the party of your choice. If elected (and it is possible) you will be in a powerful position to be able to help animals in your area, maybe protecting a wildlife area against development by a supermarket chain, or campaigning to prevent local pet shops from stocking birds. Make your concern about animals clear when you stand for election; there are many people – especially younger voters – who will share it and be only too happy to help put you in a position when you can do something positive.

RESOURCE

- *Animals and Cruelty and Law* by Noël Sweeney (from Alibi, P.O. Box 707, Bristol BS99 1FT; price £6.95 plus £1 p&p). An important reference book for anyone trying to come to grips with what the law does and does not allow, and how animals get a poor deal out of it anyway.

28

INVEST IN COMPASSION

Whenever people say, 'We mustn't be sentimental, you can take it they are about to do something cruel. And if they add, 'We must be realistic,' they mean they are going to make money out of it.

BRIGID BROPHY

They used to say that knowledge is power. I used to think so, but I now know that they mean money.

LORD BYRON (1788—1824).

BACKGROUND

Until recently, the debate about the corporate use of animals existed almost entirely outside the institutions responsible for using the animals. More recently, however, concern about animal abuse has spread to people in all walks of life – including those who have money to invest. As shareholders stop and think before they place their money, companies are being forced to reconsider the ways in which they are running their business.

The power of the shareholder is, of course, immense. In the USA, in 1985, it was shareholders who set in motion a legal wrangle that eventually forced Iroquois Brands company to include an animal rights resolution in its proxy statement concerning the force-feeding of geese to make liver pâté.

Starting in 1987, People for the Ethical Treatment of Animals (PETA) began using shareholder resolutions to gain official admission to the annual meetings of nine major companies to protest against their use of animals, and, in 1990, shareholder resolutions began to be used for animal issues other than product testing. PETA submitted a resolution to American Express in 1990, seeking a ban on its fur sales; the American Society for the Prevention of Cruelty to Animals (ASPCA) submitted challenges to factory farming to McDonald's and Pepsico (owner of Kentucky Fried Chicken, Taco Bell and

Pizza Hut). A recent report by the Investor Responsibility Research Center found that six of the nine companies targeted by animal rights organisations had reduced the number of animals they used by an average of 42 per cent between 1986 and 1988.

YOUR MONEY – THEIR LIVES

If you have money to invest, think carefully before you do so. How you eventually choose to place it could actually save animal lives. There are various ways that you can do this:

- *Ethical investments*: Invest in a company with which you're familiar, which you *know* shares your concerns about animals, and which has a policy of avoiding cruelty at all costs. Such companies might include ones making vegan foods, cruelty-free cosmetics or household products. If you are drawn to one in particular, but are not quite sure about its business practices, don't forget that as a potential shareholder you have the right to ask questions first!
- You may prefer to let someone else do the checking. There are now a couple of companies which will handle ethical investing for you. The Ethical Investment Fund originally only handled lump sum investments, but it now also includes a savings plan which caters for those who wish to make regular savings. Contact them for details at 10 Queen Street, London W1X 7PD; tel. (071) 491 0558. Another company offering advice on making ethically and ecologically sound investments is West Anglia Brokers Ltd, Station Road, Kirton, Boston, Lincolnshire PE20 1EF; tel. (0205) 723898. A growing number of independent stockbrokers are now also acting to steer investors away from companies exploiting animals; seek them out. (And if you're one of them, make sure potential clients know how to find you!)
- Alternatively, buy stock in a company that still abuses animals, then use your position to help change company policy. The first step is to pressure such companies into disclosing detailed (and often closely guarded) information to shareholders regarding their use of animals. Then make sure this information is no longer hush-hush – not just as far

as other shareholders are concerned, but the rest of the world too. Next put forward a proposal asking for a ban on any practices you consider to be exploitative. Not as easy as it sounds – but by working from the inside you have a better chance of being heard.

Other Ways to Make Money Talk

- *Credit where credit is due:* Your choice of credit card can help animals too. If you own an American Express card, for example, but feel strongly about getting the company to stop selling furs, write and resign, saying that you will renew membership when the company makes a commitment to fur-bearing animals and caring (ex)cardholders.
- There are now a wide range of credit cards available that are linked in with societies formed to help animals; a small amount of the money from each purchase made with the card goes to the relevant society. These include Care for the Wild, the Royal Society for the Protection of Birds (RSPB), the National Canine Defence League, and others. A plus is that the eyecatching designs get you into discussions with sales people!

29

CORPORATE CRUELTY: FIVE AT A TIME

I definitely think large corporations are capable of doing good, but many of them are locked into old habits. Corporations are just like people: they often need to be jolted out of comfortable practices. That's what we're doing with cosmetics companies that test their products on animals – increasing their discomfort level.

SUSAN RICH, in Phil Maggitti's 'Susan Rich: Compassion Begins in the Home', *The Animals' Agenda*, May 1990

THE PROBLEM

We were hard-pressed to pick the worst five – just five – corporations to reprimand for their treatment of animals in the laboratory. But, in the interest of space and convenience, we did limit our list to a chosen few and provide for you here the names, addresses and phone numbers of five organisations considered currently in the winners' circle when it comes to deserving some focused public heat. More and more people are calling upon them and businesses like them to develop a conscience. In the cosmetics industry, that means acknowledging that other-than-humans are not ours to experiment on, and then seeking and using better ways to test products. These five multi-national giants are in a position to set the trend.

THE SOLUTION

Petition, write to the president of each company, call, boycott, and return products (most companies have unconditional, money-back guarantees) to the following:

- L'Oréal, Centre Eugène Schueller, 41 Rue Martre, 92117 Clichy, France.

UK address: L'Oréal, 30 Kensington Church Street, London W8 4HA.

○ *Products*: L'Oréal make-up and hair-care products, Studio Line, Performing Preference hair dyes, Paloma Picasso perfumes, Ambre Solaire suntan lotion; also, Lancôme cosmetics.

○ People are learning that the world's most profitable cosmetics company is also one of the cruellest. To date, L'Oréal won't agree to stop poisoning and killing animals, even though non-animal tests are now in use by more than 300 'cruelty-free' companies.

○ L'Oréal claims 'only' 5 per cent of its products are tested on animals. Given that other major companies, such as Avon, Estée Lauder, and Revlon have given up animal tests altogether, it should not be so difficult for L'Oréal to follow suit.

○ L'Oréal executive vice-president James Nixon, who is in a position to change his company's cosmetics testing practices, has said, 'I'm not a scientist, but the tests sound crazy to me.' Still, he has resisted taking a stand against the tests.

○ L'Oréal has tried to console people concerned about their animal testing by telling them they test 'only' on rats and mice – thereby minimising the importance of animals known to be as sentient as any others.

○ One of L'Oréal's sunscreen product tests involved frying live hairless mice wrapped in foil.

● The Gillette Co., Prudential Tower Building, Boston, MA 02199, USA.

UK address: Gillette UK Ltd, Great West Road, Isleworth, Middlesex PW7 5NP.

● *Products:* In addition to its razors and blades (including the Sensor razor, which the company recently introduced), Gillette makes such toiletries and cosmetics as Right Guard deodorant, Foamy brand shaving cream, Silkience shampoo, Toni Home Perms, and Aapri and Jafra cosmetics, their only line *not* tested on animals. The company also sells Liquid Paper correction fluid and Paper Mate and Flair pens.

When Gillette's testing practices were first exposed in

1985, so many customers returned their products that Gillette has since changed its refund policy. To receive a refund, complainants to Gillette must currently state, 'I find the performance of these Gillette products to be unsatisfactory, and I am demanding a full refund.' (Be sure to tell them that you have found a wonderful cruelty-free brand to use in their product's place.) Be warned that Gillette will not now refund products to people complaining about its testing on other-than-human-beings. Still, you might try ending your refund request letter with, 'PS: I also think you should stop testing your products on animals, and I will not try your products again until you do so.' Environmental organisations for anti-apartheid groups have joined animal rights organisations in an international boycott of Gillette, in protest at the company's 'irresponsible social practices'. At an April 1990 protest at Gillette's world headquarters in Boston, USA, demonstrators presented the company with the 'Green Genie Bad Neighbor Award', reprimanding Gillette for its continued air and water pollution, production of petroleum-based plastic materials, use of animals in product testing, and refusal to divest holdings in South Africa.

● Johnson & Johnson, 1 Johnson & Johnson Plaza, New Brunswick, NJ 08933, USA.

UK address: Johnson & Johnson Ltd, Foundation Park, Rocksborough Way, Maidenhead, Berkshire SL5 9EY.

○ *Products*: Baby shampoo, Sundown sunscreen, Shower-to-Shower Body Powder, Stayfree and Carefree feminine hygiene products.

○ J&J reported in spring 1989 that animal use for non-medical consumer products had dropped 80 per cent since 1983, 'including animals used in eye and skin irritation studies', but it has not substantiated this figure.

○ One of J&J's best-known products is its 'no more tears' baby shampoo. But really, no amount of animal testing can make it desirable to put any shampoo in the eye. Mothers today recall experiencing – and seeing their own children now experience – a *large* amount of tears and pain when accidentally getting Johnson's Baby Shampoo in the eyes.

- Chesebrough-Ponds, Inc., 33 Benedict Place, Greenwich, Connecticut 06830, USA.

  UK address: Chesebrough-Ponds Ltd, P.O. Box 1DY, Hesket House, Portman Square, London W1A 1DY.

  ○ *Products:* Cutex nail polish remover; Pond's beauty creams, lotions and bars; Rave hair-care products; Vaseline products; Aim; Close-up, Pepsodent and Signal; Impulse; Prince Matchabelli division (Aziza cosmetics, Erno Laszlo skin care); and a recently acquired Fabergé division (which, to date, will not sign a Statement of Assurance that it does not test on animals).

  ○ As companies such as Chesebrough-Ponds are trying to assure customers that they are taking measures to reduce and eliminate the use of animals in product testing, the actual amount of testing elsewhere is on the rise. According to an article in the *Toronto Star* ('Cosmetics firms up research spending'): 'The beauty industry, founded on image and marketing, is turning more and more to science to give sales a boost,' wrote Elizabeth Collier. It is in the name of science that so many animal tests are done – 'new' and 'improved' products almost invariably mean more animal tests.

- Clairol, Inc. (division of Bristol-Myers), 345 Park Avenue, New York, NY 10154, USA.

  UK address: Bristol-Myers Co. Ltd, Clairol Division, The Avenue, Egham, Surrey TW20 9AB.

  ○ *Products:* Final Net hair spray, Sea Breeze, Condition hair products, and the following hair dyes: Nice 'n Easy, Miss Clairol, Loving Care, and Ultress.

  ○ Clairol's own materials and data demonstrate that safety is clearly not the reason it uses the Draize eye-irritancy test; if it were, products that were Draize-tested and caused eye injury would not be marketed. Instead, information Clairol itself has released reveals that many of the products it markets are acknowledged eye irritants, and some can cause permanent eye damage. (Clairol's notice regarding its permanent hair colours reads, 'CAUTION. Eye irritants . . . the mixture may cause severe irritation and possible permanent eye injury.')

O Testing cosmetics on other-than-human beings is not necessary for caution labelling (a general-purpose label should be mandatory on all potentially harmful products). Neither is it contributing to knowledge about how to treat eye injuries – animals are not treated but simply killed after a test, or 'recycled' into more tests.

O Clairol's Dr John Corbitt has claimed that the often painful Dermal Skin Test causes no more discomfort to animals than a man feels when shaving.

O Erwin Whitman, MD, Bristol-Myers' Vice-President of medical affairs, has said, 'If we only look at it from the point of view of efficiency and economy, we are much better off doing anything we do *in vitro* (non-animal) than in animals because it's a cheaper, it's quicker, more reliable, there's less variation – everything about it is better.' Clairol would do well to follow his advice.

Note: Boycotts are most effective when enacted *en masse*! Circulate a petition in your neighbourhood, office and/or school. Collect products and return them in a large package addressed to the company's chairperson. Be sure to let the company know what and why you are boycotting.

30

MIND YOUR 'BEES' AND 'SHREWS'

> Dismembering animals begins with dismembering language.
>
> Columnist COLMAN MCCARTHY

> The man who is described as behaving 'like a beast' would often in his behavior be a disgrace to any known animal.
>
> ERNEST BELL

THE PROBLEM

'Words, words, words,' mused Shakespeare. No one can dispute their importance, and yet we use them with an alarming lack of care.

Best-selling author and self-described 'curmudgeon' Cleveland Amory points out that we often insult each other by calling each other animal names such as 'pig', 'swine', 'weasel', 'skunk', or 'jackass'. We berate each other by using animal similes such as 'mean as a snake', 'stubborn as a mule', 'cunning as a fox', and 'silly as a goose'. One person ridicules another with terms like 'chicken', 'bull-headed', or 'dumb bunny'; and a questionable situation is 'fishy'. Derogatory words for *women* too include 'dog', 'cow', 'shrew', 'vixen' and 'bitch'. Amory notes that one dictionary definition for *animal* is 'a bestial person'.

Unthinkingly, we develop callousness and indifference to animals by using language that is euphemistic, inaccurate, and deceptive. We label the flesh cut from animal corpses as 'meat', 'veal', 'pork', 'beef', and 'poultry'. The meat industry, endeavouring to improve the image of their product, have come up with even more imaginative cover-ups. 'Maternity unit' is the farrowing crate where pigs are confined for up to three weeks, unable to turn around. A 'pig nursery' refers to the multi-tier cage where young piglets are put after weaning. The place where chickens are slaughtered has become a 'poultry processing plant'. As author Carol Adams writes, we have 'institutionalised the oppression of animals on at least two levels: in formal structures such as slaughterhouses, meat markets, zoos, laboratories, and circuses, and through our language.'

THE SOLUTION

Liberate your language. Colman McCarthy writes, 'Language shapes attitudes and attitudes shape behavior.' As our society attempts to cleanse itself of racist and sexist language, so, too, must we become aware and get rid of speciesist language – adopting a vocabulary that is accurate and dignifying to other-than-human beings. The Blacker Group for Animal Rights, a grass-roots group in the north-east of the US, offers the following tips to help us choose our words carefully;

- Refer to all individuals with gender as 'he' or 'she', and never 'it'. ('It' refers only to inanimate objects.) Likewise, other-than-humans are 'living *beings*' rather than 'living *things*', and we should refer to them with the relative pronoun 'who' rather than 'which'.
- Use 'companion' in lieu of 'pet'; and 'guardian', 'protector', or 'friend' in place of 'owner' and 'master'.
- Use honest and accurate language when referring to suffering and death. The terms 'put to sleep', 'sacrifice', and 'harvest' are euphemisms for 'destroy', 'kill' – or 'murder' (unless the act is truly *euthanasia*, which Webster's dictionary describes as 'the act or practice of killing for reasons of mercy').

31

FIRST AID: BE PREPARED FOR ANIMAL EMERGENCIES

All the arguments to prove man's superiority cannot shatter this hard fact: in suffering the animals are our equals.

PETER SINGER, *Animal Liberation*

To help life reach full development, the good [person] is a friend of all living things.

ALBERT SCHWEITZER, *The Thoughts of Albert Schweitzer*

There is no doubt that much of what we know of medicine comes . . . from the birds and animals that we have watched . . . We have long known and used much that the birds and beasts have taught us . . . Animals go without any mystical query to the water or mud or herb that will help them, and as far as we can tell they do not question their going, nor pray to be led, nor offer their thanks when they are better. Neither do they need our aid, except of course when we have caged and domesticated them past their own help. But we need them and learn ceaselessly from them.

M.F.K. FISHER, *A Cordiall Water: A Garland of Odd and Old Receipts to Assuage the Ills of Man & Beast*

THE PROBLEM

Few humans get through life illness- and accident-free. The same is true, of course, for other-than-human beings. Just in case someone needs your help, it's a good idea to know some basic emergency-response techniques and what to watch for.

THE SOLUTION

• In case of emergency, seek veterinary help right away.

Describe symptoms or injuries clearly, and take careful note of instructions. Generally, keep the victim quiet and still; in the case of traffic accidents, move victims carefully and gently out of danger, and then follow these procedures: When waiting for a vet the general principle is to stop any bleeding (without cutting off circulation), and keep air passages clear of obstructions while disturbing the animal as little as possible. If you need to carry an injured dog, make a stretcher out of a blanket, board, coat, or sack; put it on the ground and gradually slide it under him or her. Keep the stretcher taut. Stem bleeding with a clean handkerchief, piece of sheet or any cloth by making a pad and securing it to the wound, then elevate the injured body part.

- Always carry emergency numbers of veterinarians in your wallet and keep them stuck to the telephone at home.

- Two other contact phone numbers you should never go without are those of your local RSPCA office, and the twenty-four-hour emergency number of the National Animal Rescue Association – (0604) 647552. Both will offer help and/or advice in any emergency situation: whether it is a cow trapped in mud, a swan who has swallowed a fishing line, a dog down a pothole. Do, however, remember that they are extremely busy and contact them only if absolutely necessary.

- Injured animals, however familiar, may snap or bite out of fear and pain. A bandage or belt can be used as a makeshift muzzle, looped around the snout a couple of times and then tied behind the head. Make sure animals can breathe easily (watch out for heaving sides, a sign of breathing difficulty) and aren't vomiting or they may choke. Release the muzzle as soon as you can.

- Shock is a basic problem with any form of trauma; keep animals as quiet and warm as possible. If possible, put one person strictly in charge of monitoring the animal.

- Carry Bach Flower Rescue Remedy in case of emergency (available from Bach Flower Remedies Ltd, The Bach Centre, Mount Vernon, Sotwell, Wallingford, Oxon, OX10 0PZ). A few drops on the lips is calming, and the remedy is effective for both humans and other-than-humans.

- *Beware*: Human medicines may not be suitable for other-than-humans, and some can have disastrous results – aspirin, for example, can be fatal to cats, Nurofen can damage the liver of dogs. The therapeutic needs of other-than-human beings can also be quite different from ours, due to physiological differences. Since rats and horses cannot vomit, giving them something to induce vomiting may make the situation worse. Always check with a vet first.
- The following symptoms, in any combination, should always be taken very seriously:
    - Bleeding from any orifice: nose, mouth, ears, rectum, sex organs
    - Any problems with eyes: watering or half-closed, third eyelid exposed
    - Straining to urinate or repeated trips to the litterbox
    - Bloating or collapse after eating, exercise, or rapid intake of water
    - Unusually lethargic or agitated behaviour
    - Drinking lots of water
    - Fur standing on end
    - Loss of appetite
    - Continuous vomiting
    - Dragging or holding limbs
    - Sudden weight loss
    - Diarrhoea
    - Coughing
    - Lumps
- Advice for particular problems:
    - *Choking*: Try to look in the mouth, and check the tongue, roof of the mouth, teeth and gums. Holding the tongue with a handkerchief will make looking down the throat easier. If you see any objects stuck (i.e sticks, bones, small balls) try very gently to get them out, but be careful; most will have to be removed by the vet under anaesthetic. If you cannot reach the object, hold your companion upside down and shake him or her. A sharp blow on the back of the neck or between the shoulders will sometimes dislodge a blunt object from the throat. Get to a vet ASAP. As a last resort, place your hands on either side of your

companion's rib cage, then give him/her a very quick, firm squeeze to rapidly compress the lungs. If administered incorrectly, it can cause additional injuries, so ask your veterinarian to demonstrate the proper method to use for your companion animal.

- *When your companion animal stops breathing*: Artificial respiration and cardio-pulmonary resuscitation (CPR) may be required if your friend stops breathing. To give artificial resuscitation, clear a cat's or dog's mouth of any foreign matter, and then close it. Cover his or her nostrils with a clean, thin cloth or gauze. Exhale directly into the nostrils twelve to fifteen breaths per minute. If the heart is not beating, it may be necessary to concurrently conduct CPR. Get someone to transport you and your companion animal to the veterinarian's surgery while you are performing CPR. Ask your veterinarian to demonstrate the proper procedure for your companion animal.

  O *Drowning*: Swing a small animal gently upside down by the hind legs to evacuate the water inside, and apply mouth-to-mouth resuscitation, if necessary.

  O *(Suspected) Poisoning:* Since some animals are physiologically unable to vomit, get clear instructions for an antidote from a veterinarian familiar with the species.

  O *Heat stroke*: First get the animal out of the sun and heat. Then the animal should be quickly hosed down, placed in a tub of cool water, or wrapped in wet rags until the body temperature is lowered. Finally, treat for shock and/or get a vet to administer intravenous fluids, if necessary.

RESOURCES

- *Care for the Wild* is a book that tells you exactly how to do just that. Attractive, easy to use, and covering a wide range of emergency situations, it costs £4.95 and is available from Care for the Wild, 1 Ashfolds, Horsham Road, Rusper, Horsham, West Sussex RH12 4QX.
- *Animal First Aid* by Rorke Garfield, published by and available from the National Animal Rescue Association, 21 Highlands Avenue, Spinney Hill, Northampton NN3 1BG (price £2.25). Full of tips to help you cope with such problems

as getting out injured wild animals who have dug themselves in under a shed, birds down the chimney, what to feed an orphan fox or badger cub.

32

IMPROVING A DOG'S LIFE

My little old dog;
A heart-beat at my feet.
EDITH WHARTON, from 'A Lyrical Epigram'
(as quoted in *The Extended Circle*,
by Jon Wynne-Tyson)

Pets, like kings' favourites, are usually the recipients of an abundance of sentimental affection but of little real kindness; so much easier is it to give temporary caresses than substantial justice.
HENRY S. SALT, *Animals' Rights*

'Only Her Feline Friend Would Know': according to *Harper's* 'Index', 57 per cent of cat 'owners' say they confide in their cats about important matters.

THE PROBLEM

Food, shelter, and water do not a life make – at least not a great life. 'Environmental enrichment' is the new term for what is now recognised as being equally important to all animals: in other words, love, affection, interesting activities, and the knowledge that they are important to someone. Too many animals merely exist in human homes, loved in the back of busy people's minds, but benignly neglected.

THE SOLUTION

Give your other-than-human companion a gift (or two or three) that will make her or him happier.

- *Quality time*: To turn off that television and resolve to walk and play daily with your faithful companion animal is the best present of all. For birds, rabbits, hamsters, gerbils, and other caged-for-safety companions, daily open-door time with you, in an accident-proof room, is a must.
- *Interspecies communication*: Does your 'interaction' with your dog consist only of reprimands? Is your side of the 'conversation' limited to commands, such as 'sit', 'stay', 'down', 'shut up', and 'stop it'? According to PETA librarian Karen Porreca, animals try to communicate with us all the time. She writes:

    It's important to pay attention to your dog's body language – his or her primary means of getting through to you. A stare, a wag of the tail, a paw on your knee, a whimper – ignoring these 'remarks' is tantamount to ignoring your friend's 'hello' or 'I'm in need of something.' Even if you do nothing more than wink or make a reassuring clucking sound or say, 'I see you,' at least you've acknowledged your dog's communication.

    Dogs also have a wide range of vocal expressions. In addition to whines, whimpers and growls, they have quite a variety of different barks. By paying close attention you will quickly learn the difference between barks that mean 'I'm so happy to see you' and 'There's a cat outside the window' and 'I'm having fun playing' and 'There's a strange human at the door.' Understanding your dog's message gives you the opportunity to respond appropriately.

- *A room with a view!* A cat or dog window perch or ramp to relieve the boredom of wall-watching.
- *A dog/cat door* (into a fenced yard, of course): For relief of a different, more urgent sort – no one expects *human* beings to keep their legs crossed for eight to ten hours a day! If cats can come and go unattended, be sure to safeguard Tiddles by

adding a 45-degree interior angle to the top of your fencing. Cats and cars don't mix.

- *A permanent house guest:* Dogs are pack animals, so don't let your companion's world consist of you, and only you. After all, you're not always home and can never *fully* understand subtle canine lingo and needs. A companion from the local pound can make a world of difference.

- *Something to chew:* Tennis balls and rubber, rope or nylon (*not* rawhide) chew toys.

- *A foam pad to rest and sleep on:* It keeps dogs and cats out of draughts and provides relief from arthritis and protection for joints, especially older ones. If your cat or dog likes to chew, cover the pad with a really strong fabric like denim.

- *A kiddie swimming pool:* Cool relief for dogs in the summer. (If other small mammals inhabit your garden, keep a stone or brick in the pool at the edge to make sure any animals that fall in can also climb out.)

- *Your patience:* Never scold your dog for not understanding you. Writes PETA's Porreca:

  It's important to actively teach your dogs the things you want them to understand. Imagine how you would feel if someone who had some kind of 'power' over you (such as your boss or your parents, when you were little) told you to do something, using words that you couldn't understand, and then punished or scolded you when you didn't do it. Or suppose you were trying to learn a foreign language and the teacher kept changing the meanings of the words, so that it was impossible for you to learn them. This is what we do to our companion dogs when we expect them to understand English without ever having been taught any. It's unfair to them and very distressing.

- There are various toys now on the market for cats, but most of them still prefer the piece of paper you've screwed up and are just about to throw into the bin! Of course, having you throw it for them (repeatedly, if possible) is even better. A longer-lasting alternative is a ping-pong ball. Though cats are without doubt more self-sufficient than dogs, don't neglect your cat friend. Feeding him or her regularly is not enough. Leaving cats alone for hours, neglecting to play with them or make a fuss of them, is cruelty of a more subtle kind, but cruelty just the same.

- *A flexi-leash:* Retracting leash with braking and locking device that helps reduce pulling and tugging, makes walking the dog safer and easier. Available at most pet supply shops or by mail from numerous catalogues. The National Canine Defence League (1 Pratt Mews, London NW1 0AD) sells them in various sizes – buy from them and help support their work.

RECREATIONAL READING

- Like to know why dogs chase their tails? Why cats' teeth sometimes chatter? Two excellent books that will help you understand cats and dogs better than ever before are *Dogwatching* (1986) and *Catwatching* (1986), both by Desmond Morris and published by Jonathan Cape.

33

'RATS!' (. . . AND OTHER RODENTS)

None of our fellow mortals is safe who eats what we eat, who in any way interferes with our pleasures, or who may be used for work or food, clothing or ornament, or mere cruel, sportish amusement. Fortunately many are too small to be seen, and therefore enjoy life beyond our reach. And . . . it is a great comfort to learn that vast multitudes of creatures, great and small and infinite in number, lived and had a good time . . . before man [existed].

JOHN MUIR,
'Stickeen: An Adventure with a Dog and a Glacier'

It is much easier to arouse sympathy for dogs, cats and primates . . . but, ultimately it may be the lowly rat who truly tests if humanity is worthy of extending its presence to new realms. There may be no greater example of the withholding of compassion to a whole species than our present treatment of the domesticated rat.

DANIEL VAN ARSDALE
(courtesy Buddhists Concerned for Animals)

THE PROBLEM

Finding rodent droppings, hearing the patter of little feet, and noticing the corner of your library book has been chewed can pose a dilemma for people who care about animals. Most find it untenable to put up with indoor rodents but feel equally strongly that 'exterminating' them is out of the question. Traditional methods of rodent control like poisons and anti-coagulants inflict enormous suffering on these little beings who are certainly as capable of suffering as any other animal, and who are only trying to survive. Fortunately, alternatives exist.

Rat Fact

Number of reported cases of humans bitten by rats in New York City in 1985: 311. Number reported bitten by other people: 1,519 (*Harper's* 'Index')

THE SOLUTION

While we may not want to sign over our lease to the local mice and rats, we can discourage their tenancy or effect their relocation in as humane and civilised a manner as possible. Some guidelines:

- Indoor rodent infestation is largely *preventable* by maintaining clean, sanitary conditions. Dry up the food supply and your visiting rat family will have to go out to eat. Do not leave human, dog, or cat food lying around. Sweep and wipe up crumbs, and put left-overs away. Store dry goods such as rice, birdseed, biscuits, breakfast cereals, and flour in sealed containers made of metal, glass, or ceramic with tight-fitting lids rather than in paper or plastic bags. Keep fruits and vegetables in the refrigerator.

- Plug holes or cracks where mice or rats might enter or re-enter with mesh or tar paper, then plaster over the top.

- Many farmers keep cats as a form of mouse and rat control, though the idea of having a cat around specifically to do such a job is obviously not acceptable to most true animal lovers. It seems, however, that there is some truth in the idea that even the hated smell of cats will be enough to put rodents off the idea of sharing your home. (Mice also – it is said – dislike intensely the smell of mint, camomile, oleander, and tar!)

- If nothing else seems to work and you're getting desperate, use a humane mousetrap from the National Centre for Alternative Technology, Machynlleth, Powys, Wales, SY20 9AZ; tel. (0654) 2440. This consists of a well ventilated plastic box with a spring-release trap door that shuts once the rodent enters in search of food. The trap can then be taken outdoors where s/he can be released unharmed. It's a good idea to put some shredded newspaper in with the bait; this will give a bored mouse something to play with, and an especially timid one will be able to snuggle down and hide beneath it. Just the same, check your trap sixteen billion times a day! (Wild animals in traps experience extreme distress and can even injure themselves attempting to get free.)

- *Never* use a glue trap. Rodents caught in glue traps can struggle for days before they are found and are frequently thrown into the rubbish bin alive. Trapped animals, struggling to free themselves, often pull out their own hair and sometimes bite off their legs. The glue causes their eyes to become badly irritated and swollen, and those whose faces get stuck in it slowly suffocate. All trapped animals experience stress, trauma, and dehydration. In fact, few shops sell glue traps, the majority offering the spring loaded kind designed to break the mouse's back or neck. Though these can result in a quick death, this is by no means guaranteed; the victim can live on, struggling to break free, for hours.

- If your local stores sell glue or spring loaded traps, and/or poison for rats and mice, please complain in person to the manager, and suggest they stock humane alternatives instead.

34

NO SKIN OFF THEIR BACKS

To my mind the life of the lamb is no less precious than that of a human being. I should be unwilling to take the life of the lamb for the sake of the human body. I hold that, the more helpless a creature, the more entitled it is to protection by man from the cruelty of man.

MOHANDAS K. GANDHI,
An Autobiography: The Story of My Experiments

In the USA, a May 1990 poll in *Parents Magazine* (Vol. 65, No. 5, p. 33) indicated that 69 per cent of people polled considered themselves against killing animals for leather – 46 per cent of whom said it should be illegal.

THE PROBLEM

In Australia, it's not the bloody fur trade they have to combat, it's the wool industry; yet, in this country we are oblivious to the massive suffering of sheep on foreign mega-farms. Most of us are equally unaware of the suffering stitched into each silk blouse, down pillow, and pair of leather shoes, derived from slaughterhouse activity on our own turf. The garment industry has changed dramatically over the years: animal-derived clothing has meant increased cruelties due to factory farming practices, while natural fibre and synthetics have become increasingly 'cool'. Nowadays, given a heightened awareness and an eye for 'compassionate clothing', no one has to dress like a Neanderthal cave-dweller to look great and feel comfortable.

Leather Logic

● Leather, like fur, is the skin of once-living animals, and, really, who wants to wear that? Unfortunately, leather has had a reputation of being elegant and stylish; the leather industry is worth £650 million a year in Britain alone. Yet the trend is shifting as people recognise that because leather is a slaughterhouse by-product, buying and wearing it directly supports the factory-farming industry and its systematic, mass animal exploitation.

- Leather, in fact, subsidises the meat industry. The majority of the profit comes not from the meat but from the parts that cannot be eaten such as bones and hooves (made into gelatine), the blood (used in pet food, fertilisers, and pharmaceuticals) and the hide, which can account for up to 50 per cent of the total value of an animal. Some slaughter-houses even have their own tanneries. When dairy cows' production declines, their skin is also made into leather; and the hides of their offspring, veal calves, are made into high-priced calfskin. Luxury suede may be made from the skin of unborn calves.

- According to the Tanners' Council of America's *US Leather Industry Statistics*, every year, approximately 230 million cattle, 350 million sheep, 175 million goats, and 700 million pigs, are slaughtered worldwide for their flesh and skin.

- Most of the leather produced and sold in Britain is made from skins of cattle, calves and pigs, but leather is also made from the hides of horses, sheep, lambs, goats, and kids slaughtered for meat. Myriad other species around the world are hunted and killed specifically for their skins, including zebras, buffaloes, deer, kangaroos, tigers, ostriches, eels, sharks, whales, seals, frogs, crocodiles, mules, and lizards. Up to one-third of 'exotic' leathers come from endangered, illegally poached animals.

- Beauty Without Cruelty in India reported that stray dogs are being caught, killed by electrocution, and their skins being made into leather products, some of which may well end up back in Britain. Saddles and golf bags made from elephant hides can still be purchased at Harrods in London.

- All animal-skin products imply suffering.

  ○ Reptiles such as alligators and snakes are usually conscious when skinned to make shoes, handbags, and belts, because no one can be bothered or wants to incur the extra expense involved in stunning them. Cold-blooded reptiles also take far longer to die than mammals – hours, sometimes days.

O To produce 'kid' gloves, young Karakul goats are boiled alive by shepherds because that tenderises the skin.

O Wildlife in rivers and streams are killed by toxic chemicals dumped by the leather-tanning industry. There are also human health consequences: the Centers for Disease Control found that the incidence of leukaemia among residents in an area surrounding one tannery in Kentucky, USA, was five times the national average.

What's Wrong With Wool?

- Wool is the sheared coat of sheep. Breeders have created sheep called Merinos, who are extremely wrinkly (more wrinkles mean more wool). This unnatural overload of wool causes many sheep to die of heat exhaustion in the summer, as well as of exposure to cold and damp after late shearing in the autumn (a closely shorn sheep is more sensitive to cold than even a naked human, since a sheep's normal body temperature is much higher than ours). In Australia (where 70 per cent of all wool used in clothing originates, and where about 175 million sheep are raised for wool and then slaughtered every year), approximately 6.3 million sheep die on the farm, and up to 10 per cent of all sheep die on their way to slaughterhouses in the Middle East – largely from exposure. (Over-production of wool and a worldwide fall in demand have resulted in a decision to kill at least 2 million sheep to avoid starvation; they are being shot and buried – preferable, many say, to being exported *en masse* to satisfy the Arab appetite for sheep flesh.)
- One of the worst and most painful wool industry practices is 'mulesing': slicing off large sections of the lamb's backsides (skin, not wool) with shears, and *without* anaesthesia. Farmers employ this practice because the bloody wound, when and if it heals three to five painful weeks later, will pull the skin tight and prevent moisture and urine from collecting in the (artificially wrinkly) Merino sheep's skin, which otherwise is a haven for blowflies and their eggs.
- Sheep are violently pinned down and often get cut from the rough shearing that is inevitable when speed means money. Farmers use a hot tar compound to seal bleeding wounds,

which are especially prevalent on farms where computer-
controlled shearing machinery holds the sheeps' faces in a
clamp, while a sensor directs a shearing comb that can fail to
circumvent teats and other protrusions.

- Lambs endure ear-punching, tail-docking (having their tails
cut off), and castration; and ageing sheep are subjected to
'tooth-grinding', a procedure in which unanaesthetised
sheep are restrained and have their teeth cut down to the
gums, exposing the sensitive pulp cavities inside.

- Millions of sheep are exported live to the Middle East each
year by ship. Packed tightly together in huge transporters,
they travel great distances and for weeks are forced to stand
in (and eat food tainted by) urine and faeces. Those who
arrive alive are slaughtered by having their throats slit while
still conscious.

- Much of the wool from British-reared sheep is skin wool
obtained from slaughtered lambs and hoggets (between
weaning and first shearing). One of the major problems these
genetically engineered and disease prone animals suffer from
is foot rot. The hoof may actually fall off, leaving the animal
in such pain that he/she will drop to his/her knees to feed,
dragging along the ground to reach more food; if not treated,
eventually the animal will die from exhaustion.

Down Is Out

- Down is the insulating feathers of ducks and geese. Most
down in pillows, parkas and duvets comes from birds who
have endured a life of preparation for the slaughterhouse.
The rest derives from geese raised for down; and anyone who
has plucked her or his eyebrows can (only begin to) imagine
how painful it is for these animals to have all their feathers
pulled from their necks and breasts – not just once, but four
or five times during their short lives.

So Is Silk!

- Silk comes from the shiny fibre that a silkworm makes to
form the cocoon from which, sixteen days later, he or she
should emerge transformed into a beautiful moth. Many
people think of silk as 'natural', not realising that farmers

boil, steam, electrocute or microwave the silkworms alive in their cocoons by the thousands. (The International Silk Association states in its brochure, 'What is Silk?' that 'it is necessary to destroy the worm inside the cocoon if the silk is to be reeled. This is done by stifling it with heat.') It is well established that silkworms feel pain.

WHAT YOU CAN DO

- Purchase only non-leather shoes, clothing, and accessories (including watchstraps, footballs, upholstery, belts, etc.). Alternatives include cotton, linen, rayon, canvas, nylon, ramie, rubber, and vinyl, whose advantages include affordability and ease of cleaning. Today there many comfortable, well-made, and fashionable non-leather alternatives, such as satin dress shoes, synthetic running shoes, and canvas recreation shoes. Among other companies, Adidas; Bata; Chelsea Girl; Curtess; Dolcis; Freeman; Hardy and Willis; Lennards; Nike; Scholl; Pirelli; and Stead and Simpson have all been known to include some attractive, quality, non-leather shoes in their ranges. Look closely at your mail-order catalogues – they often have cruelty-free shoes which you'll be able to pick out easily as the material from which the shoes are made is always given. When out shopping, do not hesitate to ask salespeople for help.

- Never buy wool clothes or blankets again. Choose only cotton, synthetics, ramie, flannel, and other non-animal fibres. Their advantages are that they are not as likely to shrink, they usually cost less, they retain their bright colours longer, and they don't contribute to cruelty. Tell people – including store personnel – why you have gone cruelty-free. No one needs to steal from animals to be warm or to look good. Contact Cotton-On (29 Clifton Street, Lytham, Lancashire FY8 5HW) for their catalogue which contains clothes for men, women and children. Additionally write letters protesting against mulesing and live sheep exports to the Australian High Commission, Australia House, The Strand, London WC2B 4LU.

- Don't buy silk products. Silk is used in cloth (including taffeta), and as a colouring agent in some face powders, soaps, and other cosmetics. It can cause severe allergic skin reactions, as well as systemic reactions if inhaled or ingested. Alternatives include viscose and acetate rayon, polyesters such as Terylene and Dacron, acrylics such as Courtelle, Orlon and Dralon.

RESOURCE
● For information on fur and leather contact Campaign Against Leather and Fur (CALF), P.O. Box 17, 198 Blackstock Road, London N5.

35

A MATTER OF TASTE

But from the mountain's grassy side,
A guiltless feast I bring,
A script with herbs and fruit supplied,
And water from the spring.

OLIVER GOLDSMITH

THE PROBLEM
The reasons why we choose to eat certain foods are complex and varied. Once people ate simply to survive, eating whatever was available nearby and tasted reasonable. Today, however, many of us, particularly in the West, see food in a very different way. It is something to entertain us, to impress people with, to challenge our creativity. If the food we serve to guests at our table intrigues and amuses them, great. If it can also prove that we are cultured, well travelled and able to afford 'the best' so much the better. If it weren't for the need to impress, how many people would really choose to eat caviar, snails and frogs' legs?

In response to this need, food manufacturers and farmers are of course forging ahead to find new tastes with which to titillate our jaded palates. The result of our greed is that, once again, our other-than-human friends are the losers.

Some 'tasteless' morsels:

- Pheasant and partridges are bred specially to satisfy the demand for something different; often hand-reared, fussed over, treated like babies, they are suddenly betrayed by the very people they have come to trust – beaten out of the bushes so that a line-up of men with high-powered guns can bring them back down to the ground again. Other birds such as quail and pigeon are shot as they fly free. Hung until they begin to putrefy before being cooked, 'game birds' are a speciality commanding very high prices (the price the birds pay is even higher).

- Once venison was served only in the better-class restaurants, the meat usually coming from Scotland where the annual cull of wild deer resulted in a surplus. Now, however, deer farming is on the increase, those involved busily advertising venison as the healthy alternative to beef. At the moment there are some 300 deer farms in Britain with a breeding pool of 35,000 females; it is estimated that in ten years time – as people become used to the idea of eating 'Bambi' – there may be as many as 200,000 females. Though at present farmed deer live outside and graze naturally, some colleges are already experimenting with indoor farming, artificial insemination and 'twinning' techniques (used to increase production). Compassion in World Farming are especially concerned about slaughter techniques. Although the majority of deer are shot on the farm (or at least slaughtered on the premises), many are loaded up and transported to slaughter-houses. The distress suffered by these highly strung wild animals must be enormous; many arrive with broken legs sustained by their sheer panic.

- The 'wild' boar that is offered on restaurant menus may also be less wild than the name implies; there are thirty wild boar farms in Britain. Dormice are also being 'factory farmed'; they are lured into the traditional jar with food where, as they grow fatter, they become trapped, thereby being unable to use up calories from the food that is still being fed to them.

The result is a fat dormouse ready for slaughter in the minimum time.

- Two new concepts that haven't yet started making money for British farmers (but are expected to within a few years) are ostrich and emu farming. In both cases the farmers have purchased a small flock of birds from zoos and plan to use them as breeding stock. Commercial ostrich farming is, in fact, already widespread in Australia, and in the USA there are some 3,000 ostrich farms. Ostrich flesh, goes the publicity blurb, is rather like turkey and will make a tasty alternative for Christmas!

- Not all of the 'delicacies' the British pursue are actually produced in this country. Many are imported, the cruelty taking place so far away that it is easy to forget it ever happened. *Pâté de foie gras* originates in France; it is made from the livers of geese who have been constrained and then force fed (usually by machines) on large amounts of salted cereal so that their livers grow unnaturally large. Though many people have tried to pressure the Ministry of Agriculture to ban the import of *pâté de foie gras*, so far this has not happened. A national campaign highlighting the cruel production of frogs' legs has succeeded in persuading many supermarkets, delicatessens and restaurants to stop stocking them. (Bull frogs are cut in half while alive, the legs skinned and put aside to be frozen, the front halves thrown on to a pile and left gasping and twitching until they die, which can take as long as an hour.) The ecological disaster that followed the slaughter of millions of wild frogs in India – pests that carry disease and destroy crops suddenly multiplied – helped persuade the Indian government to ban the business, though Bangladesh and Indonesia still export vast numbers annually.

Each to His (or Her!) Own Taste

- Tastes in food are also very different from one country to another. In some parts of the world it is traditional to eat dogs, in others termites are added to the pot, or dolphins slaughtered to fill a gap on the plate. Though such tastes may seem revolting to some of us, British animals may find themselves facing long and gruelling journeys before being slaughtered in foreign abbatoirs, all in the name of profit. Though the live export trade in many animals (calves and sheep in particular) has been going on for some time, and causes the most appalling suffering to these animals, things look set to worsen in 1992 when free trade between all European Community countries comes into force. (The Treaty of Rome classifies live animals as 'agricultural products' in much the same way as fruit and vegetables, hence they can be transported under the same conditions!) The live trade in horses from Britain was stopped some years ago under the 'minimum values' clause of the 1981 Animal Health Act, which made it uneconomic to export equines to the Continent for slaughter. Now, however, this too looks likely to be resumed. Horses, ponies, donkeys and foals – some elderly, others wild, all of them cast-offs – will be herded and crushed on to overcrowded transporters to face a terrifying journey and, worse, to satisfy the continental taste for horse flesh.

THE SOLUTION

- Don't eat dead animals.
- Encourage others not to eat dead animals either. Telling them about how the animals are treated may help them to change their habits, though some people (even those who are genuinely sensitive and caring) have a knack for putting such things out of their minds. An alternative way to persuade them to stop, or at least reduce their consumption, is to take them to a really good vegetarian restaurant to show them how enjoyable animal-free food can be. Don't forget that many countries have a tradition of vegetarian cookery; try Indian, Chinese, Thai, Japanese, Malaysian, Middle Eastern, Italian and Mexican for a start.
- Learn to be creative in the kitchen; enjoy experimenting; make use of the many ingredients that are now available for vegetarians and vegans. Compile your own card file of successful recipes – other people's and your own. If you feel some lessons would be useful, and your local evening classes don't include such a course, suggest they do next term. Or contact the Vegetarian Society (UK) Ltd. (Parkdale,

Dunham Road, Altrincham, Cheshire WA14 4QG) who have got together with the South Bank Polytechnic to compile a list of meat-free courses on offer in Britain. They will also be able to tell you about the many residential learning/holidaying courses now found across the country. Like to become a qualified cook? The VS offers a Cordon Vert Diploma, many of their previous graduates going on to become chefs or open their own establishments. Again, ask for details.

- Campaign to stop local shops and restaurants offering such foods as frogs' legs and *pâté de foie gras*. Write to the manager saying that you object to their involvement in such gross cruelties to animals, and feel you would sooner buy your groceries elsewhere. Inform your local Waitrose manager that, until they stop selling venison from deer killed in slaughterhouses (they are one of the supermarkets admitting to this), you will not buy from them. Tell other people why you feel such action is justified.

- Join the many people fighting to tighten up the laws regarding the export of live animals, and to prevent the export of live equines starting up again. Get petitions signed (numerous animal rights societies are campaigning on this issue, including Compassion in World Farming, the RSPCA, the Scottish Society for the Prevention of Cruelty to Animals, and the International League for the Protection of Horses).

36

HIDDEN HORRORS: ANIMAL INGREDIENTS AND THEIR ALTERNATIVES

> At present scientists do not look for alternatives simply because they do not care enough about the animals they are using.
>
> PETER SINGER, *Animal Liberation*

THE PROBLEM

Animal bits and pieces (body fats, stomach linings, and other slaughterhouse 'by-products') often lurk in foods you'd never dream contained them, like biscuits, flour tortillas and roasted sunflower seeds, and in cosmetics and toiletries you smear on your face and rub in your hair! Brushes for blush and eye make-up are commonly made of hair from the inside of a cow's ear, shoe polish can contain cattle blood, and some toothpastes and cough medicines have rendered beef fat or tallow in them. Bandages, adhesives, wallpaper, sandpaper, and emery boards can contain bones, horns, and hooves. Home insulation and even the felt in felt-tip pens are made from hide and hair. Disheartening, isn't it?

THE SOLUTION

Unfortunately, it is still virtually impossible to eliminate all the cruelty inherent in our contemporary lifestyle, but the good news is that you can greatly reduce it by being an informed consumer.

Become a Label Reader

Learn to identify mysterious ingredients and to question chefs, waiters, doctors, nurses, beauticians, and others when in doubt.

The following objectionable ingredients range from the obvious to the obscure, but all can be easy to miss.

- *Lard*: Animal fat. Frequently used in commercially made chips, pastry and some cakes. Also in shaving creams, soaps, and cosmetics. Alternatives: pure vegetable fats or oils.
- *Suet*: Hard animal fat, usually from cows or sheep. Used for cooking such traditional dishes as Christmas pudding, mincemeat – and, of course, suet pudding! Alternatives: pure vegetable fats or oils.
- *Gelatine/gel:* Animal protein obtained from horses, cattle and pigs by boiling skin, tendons, ligaments, hooves and/or bones with water. Most commercially made jellies contain gelatine; so do most mousses; also look out for it in sweets such as marshmallows and Turkish Delight plus some ice creams and yoghurts. Sometimes an ingredient in shampoos, face masks, and other cosmetics. Serves as a coating on photographic film, vitamins, and as medicine capsules. Alternatives: agar-agar and Carageen are available in wholefood shops and make excellent jellies and desserts; pectin from fruits, dextrins, locust bean gum, and cotton gum can also be used to replace gelatine. Kosher desserts are often made without gelatine – read the labels to be sure.
- *Whey*: Milk by-product widely used in commercially made cakes, biscuits, sweets, polyunsaturated margarines, some breads, and in cheese-making. Alternative: (when necessary) soybean whey.
- *Musk*: Oil painfully obtained from the genitals of musk deer, beavers, muskrats, civet cats, and otters. Wild cats are kept captive in cages in horrible conditions, beavers are trapped, deer are shot, and cats are whipped around the genitals to produce the scented oil. Used in perfumes. Alternatives: there are many musk-type perfumes available made from plants.
- *Cochineal/carmine*: Made from the bodies of insects, cochineal is used as a red colouring in food. Carmine does the same for lipstick. Alternatives: natural food dyes (or use beetroot juice), lipsticks labelled 'cruelty-free'.
- *Placenta*: Afterbirth containing waste matter eliminated by

the foetus. Widely used in skin creams, shampoos, face masks, and other cosmetic items, placenta is derived from the uteruses of slaughtered animals. Alternatives: kelp, olive oil, wheat germ oil, coconut oil, and other vegetable oils.

- *Collagen*: A fibrous protein in vertebrates usually derived from animal tissue. Used widely in skin creams and cosmetics (when in doubt about its origin, write to the company for information). Alternatives: soy protein, almond oil, amla oil, rosemary, and nettle.
- *Lactic acid*: A slaughterhouse product, sometimes from blood and muscle tissue, produced by fermentation by certain micro-organisms. Sometimes in sauerkraut, pickles, and other food products made by bacterial fermentation. Also in some skin fresheners, where it is used as a preservative, and in plasticisers. Alternative: plant milk sugar.
- *Lactose*: Milk sugar of animals. In eye lotions, foods, tablets, cosmetics, baked goods, and medicines. Alternative: plant milk sugar.
- *Other ingredients:* Keratin, lecithin, oestrogen, progesterone, adrenalin, steroids/sterol, mink oil, fatty acids, insulin, mono- and di-glycerides.
- *Warning*: 'Natural sources', a description found on many healthfood-industry labels, especially cosmetics, can mean animal or vegetable sources. 'Natural sources' can include sources such as animal elastin, glands, fat, protein, and oil. Many ingredients can come from both animals and vegetable sources. If the label isn't specific, call or write to the company asking for details.

RESOURCES

- For a comprehensive list of cruelty-free goods (including manufactured foods, drinks, toiletries and homecare products) get *The Cruelty Free Shopper* by Lis Howlett (Bloomsbury 1989).
- BUAV's *Approved Product Guide* includes household products as well as toiletries and cosmetics. Ring their 'Choose Cruelty-Free' Hotline (071) 700 4232 for your free copy.

37

FORM A NEIGHBOURHOOD ANIMAL WATCH

I could not have slept tonight if I had left (sic) that helpless little creature perish on the ground.

ABRAHAM LINCOLN's reply to friends who chided him
for delaying them by stopping to return
a fledgling to her nest

If you pick up a starving dog and make him prosperous, he will not bite you. This is the principal difference between a dog and a man.

MARK TWAIN, *Puddin'head Wilson*

THE PROBLEM

If a baby starling falls from a nest across the road, someone's beating a dog down the street, or a squirrel gets hit by a car – what happens in your neighbourhood? On the heels of 'Neighbourhood Watch' comes 'Neighbourhood Animal Watch' – an idea first developed in the USA by caring children and then taken up by adults. There's a need for it in Britain, too. All it takes is someone to set the ball rolling.

WHAT YOU CAN DO

- You may already belong to a group or society – the Women's Institute, an exercise class, organic gardeners society or, of course, a Neighbourhood Watch Scheme – and know of animal lovers who might like to form a separate group. Put the idea to them.
- Alternatively, hold an evening or weekend meeting of neighbours who care about animals. Advertise by putting up notices in the local library and shop windows, in any community newsletter, or by hand-delivering fliers (the newspaper carrier will probably help). Find out what expertise those who attend can offer.

- Collect emergency and special-care numbers. Learn who to call in case of wildlife problems or if a companion animal goes missing, to report cruelty, and where to borrow a trap. The printed list can be distributed door-to-door. (When you find an injured wild animal, call an experienced wildlife worker immediately. Do not attempt to treat injuries yourself. Always keep injured animals safe and quiet.)

- Swap information on good and bad experiences with boarding facilities, veterinarians, groomers, 'pet sitters', and even dog product suppliers. Keep a card file for neighbours' reference.

- Develop and distribute seasonal alerts (e.g. 'Remember not to leave cloth bedding in dog houses in winter – it freezes when wet') and general tips (e.g. how to secure a water bucket, and how to make homemade biscuits for the health-conscious dog).

- 'Pet' thieves are known to use vans with blacked-out windows. Write down the registration number, colour and other details of any unfamiliar vans you may notice hanging around, just in case local cats or dogs suddenly go missing.

- Report abuse! If you witness cruelty in progress, contact your local RSPCA inspector at once. If possible, document the abuse by keeping a journal, taking photographs, and gathering eyewitness statements.

- Whether or not to try to stop the cruelty is a matter of choice, something you will have to judge for yourself at the time. Though you may be risking abuse (and even physical harm) by doing so, there are undoubtedly circumstances where you will be able to calm down the aggressor, maybe even saving the life of an animal. Youngsters stoning ducks can often be deterred from the act by a few carefully chosen words. An angry dog owner – possibly taking out her or his frustration about something completely different on the dog – may be hardly aware of what she or he is doing. If you decide to say something, be polite, calm, offering help rather than criticism.

- Though feral cats (domestic cats gone wild) are not wide-spread in Britain, colonies of them do exist, especially in cities. Feeding them from time to time is helpful, but not enough. These animals or their recent ancestors probably once lived in homes and are lost or were abandoned. They are subject to disease, starvation, injury, weather extremes, and accidents; and they need help. Borrow a humane box trap from your local animal shelter, or club together to buy one. Take the cats to the vet or the local shelter to have them examined, given the appropriate shots, and spayed or neutered, or euthanised if ill or if all adoption efforts fail. (Or contact the Cats Protection League, 17 King's Road, Horsham, West Sussex RH13 5PP for their local branch who will help both with catching and re-homing cats whenever possible.) Preventing feral cats from continuing to reproduce is the best and kindest assistance you can give them.

- When you find lost animals, your principal aim is to reunite them with their families. Check with neighbours, put up notices, ask your local newspaper about the possibility of placing a free or reduced price advertisement. Make your description less than thorough; the person looking for a lost companion should be able to describe her/him in detail. If no one responds, follow these guidelines: look for responsible people who want an animal to be a member of the family (not as a cheap guard dog or breeding machine). Ask where the animal will live, if there are other animals in the home, and how the potential guardians feel about spaying and neutering. Always check identification. Have a signed agreement that you will take the animal back if the new family cannot keep him/her. Don't be afraid to say 'no' if you are unsure. If you are unable to find a suitable home, take the animal to an RSPCA shelter, or a privately run one that you know to be good.

38

SILVER SCREAM

I don't think you should hurt or kill animals just to entertain an audience. Animals should have some rights. But there are a lot of directors, including Ingmar Bergman, who will injure animals to further a plot. I will have none of it.

The late JAMES MASON, explaining why he refused to play opposite Sophia Loren in a film containing a cock-fighting sequence

THE PROBLEM

Film-makers, even in the process of portraying animals positively, are notorious for treating them as props rather than as cast members who can get tired, hot, and sick – and who are as unable to perform bionic feats as their human counterparts. Wire-tripping, starvation, sleep deprivation, prodding, beatings, and 'tie-downs' (whereby an invisible filament is tied around, for example, a cat to force him/her to stay in place) are methods of making an animal comply with the demands of the screenplay.

Other-than-human 'actors' suffer extensive physical and psychological abuse and are virtually unprotected by law. Stress, trauma, and death are, for many, the final curtain call. Some examples:

- During the filming of a stampede scene in *The Return to Snowy River: Part II*, a pregnant mare collapsed. Approximately 100 horses were used in the scene, yet no veterinarian was present. The 'horsemen' could not determine what the problem was and decided to kill the mare. One struck her on the head with the blunt end of an axe and another sliced her jugular vein. They then dumped her body into a gully. Two other horses died in the making of the film.
- In *Earth Girls Are Easy* (1989), a live cat was thrown into a

swimming pool, and tropical fishes were thrown on to a rug to lie dying and gasping as their human counterparts joked nearby; and during the filming of *Days of Thunder* (1990), seagulls were run over by beach buggies in a chase scene on Daytona Beach after being lured to the site with food.

● A 1990 release, *In the Blood*, glorifies 'big game' hunting in a twisted homage to the late US president Theodore Roosevelt. *New York Times* reviewer Janet Maslin wrote, 'Not even those who object to violence will find themselves responding peaceably to this film . . . If anything, it is enough to make audiences wish that animals had rifles, too' (20 April 1990). The film cost thirty-one other-than-humans their lives, the first of whom was a dozing lion who had been baited by a safari leader.

● Horses were tripped with wires in *Reds*, an ox was bled at the neck in *The Killing Fields* and, in *Apocalypse Now*, a water buffalo was macheted to death. To simulate a lion being shot in *Out of Africa*, the animal was violently pulled down by the use of a cable, according to an animal trainer who worked on the set. In *The Abyss*, rats were submerged in an oxygenated liquid and later died of pneumonia-like complications. A horse was blown up and others were tripped, injured, and killed in the 1980 film *Heaven's Gate*. In addition, an illegal cock-fight was staged, and cattle and chickens were bled to get real blood to smear on actors. In *Cannibal Holocaust*, released in 1984, an opossum was slit with a knife, and a tortoise and a monkey were decapitated.

● In addition to on-screen abuse, the acquisition, care and disposal of other-than-human 'actors' raise troubling questions at a time when animal protection groups are working worldwide to protect many species from depletion due to exportation and trapping, and the complex psychological needs of other species are just beginning to be understood. Two weeks after completing the movie, *Every Which Way But Loose*, Buddha (a.k.a. Clyde), the movie's celebrated orangutan 'star', was found dead, with blood issuing from his mouth, allegedly beaten to death by his handlers. The sworn affidavit of a worker at the compound described a session of 'hitting and pounding' he witnessed one day during the filming, and other employees stated that an autopsy revealed Buddha's death was due to a cerebral haemorrhage. Orangutans are strong, but otherwise naturally solitary, intelligent forest-dwellers who are happy in Borneo, not 'on the set'.

- Films like *Rabid*, in which frightened families resort to hideous and bizarre ways to defend themselves against animals depicted as determined to bite and kill them, can inspire or fuel irrational hatred and violent acts against dogs, bats and other normally harmless creatures.

THE SOLUTION

- Avoid any film that you know or suspect includes real harm to animals. Write to the manager at the cinema where the film is showing stating why you are boycotting it; make it clear that s/he is losing a potential customer! Write also to the studio responsible for making the film explaining your objections, and asking for an assurance that they will portray animals positively in future, preferably omitting real animals from their casting calls. (Excellent realistic-looking animal models exist, and it is also possible, for example, for humans to play other-than-human primates. If *Greystoke* could use human actors costumed as chimpanzees, *Project X* did not need to use real chimpanzees. The young apes should have been left with their mothers, not bothered by trainers seen on the set carrying a sawn-off pool cue, a blackjack, and a .38-calibre pistol.)

- The majority of films shown in Britain are made in the USA or elsewhere; just a few are made in Britain. Treatment of animals during the making of British films is monitored by the RSPCA who must be informed when an animal is being used, what s/he is expected to do, and who will be caring for her or his welfare. Their basic guide includes such details as: actors should be given every opportunity to familiarise themselves with the animals in advance; no animals should be tranquillised or anaesthetised to produce an effect; animal fights should always be simulated; to obtain horse falls by tripping is prohibited. However, as it is rare for an official to attend filming, others on the set may be the only ones to see what is actually happening. Many celebrities are concerned about animal rights, as are other members of the crew. If you are concerned about the way animals were used in a specific film, write to the relevant studio requesting details. The more filmgoers do this, the more wary producers are going to be about using animals on the set.

Here are the addresses of the main film studios in the USA:

O Buena Vista Pictures Dist., Inc. (a subsidiary of Walt Disney Co.), 3900 W. Alameda Street, Burbank, CA 91505; Richard Cook, president.

O Columbia Pictures (a division of Columbia Pictures Entertainment, Inc.), Columbia Plaza, Burbank, CA 91505; Dawn Steel, president.

O MGM/UA Communications Co. (includes Metro-Goldwyn-Mayer and United Artists), 450 N. Roxbury Drive, Beverley Hills, CA 90210; Jeffrey C. Barbakow, president.

O Orion, 711 Fifth Avenue, New York, NY 10022; Arthur B. Kim, president.

O Paramount, 15 Columbus Circle, New York, NY 10023; Frank Manusco, chairman.

O Tri-Star Pictures (a unit of Columbia Pictures Entertainment, Inc.), 3400 Riverside Drive, Burbank, CA 91505; Jeffrey Sagansky, president of production.

O 20th Century-Fox Film Corp., P.O. Box 900, Beverley Hills, CA 90213; Barry Diller, chairman.

O Universal Pictures (a division of Universal City Studios and subsidiary of MCA, Inc.), 445 Park Avenue, New York, NY 10022; Thomas Pollock, vice-president of MCA, Inc., and chairman of the Motion Picture Group.

O The Walt Disney Co., 500 S. Buena Vista Street, Burbank, CA 91521; Michael D. Esner, chairman.

O Warner Brothers, Inc. (a subsidiary of Warner Communications, Inc.), 4000 Warner Boulevard, Burbank, CA 91522; Robert A. Daly, chairman.

O British film-makers are listed in the *Screen International Film and Television Year Book* (King Publications Ltd), as are film-makers from various other countries. Should you see (or hear of) a film that contains something to which you object, check the film company and then look up the address. Your local reference library will have a copy.

- If you are in a cinema and are offended at how animals are portrayed, or see a scene containing cruelty to animals, walk out! By doing so, you alert others that what happened is ethically indefensible. Let the manager know that you would not have attended if you had known there would be animal cruelty. Ask for a refund or credit note. If the explanation is firm but very polite (remember, it's not the cinema's fault), most managers will be obliging and may also learn something.
- Write and ask film critics on your local and favourite national papers to include real or perceived animal abuse in their reviews – to recognise that when a film depicts an other-than-human being in a dangerous or uncomfortable spot, it is not always safe simply to say, 'Remember, it's only a movie.'

39

SPECIOUS SOUVENIRS

If we are to save the world's wildlife, we must adopt an ethic that recognises the right of all animals to exist, places equal value on the grotesque and the spectacular, and shows as much concern for the crocodile as for the cheetah, as much for the condor as the eagle.

LEWIS REGENSTEIN, 'Animal Rights,
Endangered Species and Human Survival',
In Defense of Animals, ed. Peter Singer

What we have done to the great whales in the sacred name of commerce is an affront to human dignity, a debasement of human values and sensibility.

In the light of present knowledge of these intelligent mammals, no civilised person can contemplate the whaling industry without revulsion and shame at the insensitivity of our own species.

SIR PETER SCOTT, from an address to the
International Whaling Commission,
London, July 1979

THE PROBLEM

The USA is the world's largest consumer of endangered and exotic animal products. American superconsumers 'gobble up' products made from the teeth, feathers, shells, skins – and habitats – of species who are threatened or are in immediate danger of disappearing. Tourists return home with elephant-leg umbrella stands, ivory jewellery and carvings; sea turtle-shell guitars and hair ornaments and sea turtle skin creams; Nile crocodile-skin handbags; caiman boots; python purses; and leopard-skin coats.

Though we consume far fewer of such items in Britain (our 'collectors' are more inclined to smuggle in a rare species of parrot, or reptiles for their private zoos), we do still fuel the illegal market, often unwittingly; either we are not sure what is on the CITES (the Convention on International Trade in Endangered Species) list, or we are unable to distinguish the exact source of a souvenir. Traders are also becoming increasingly savvy in the art of 'laundering' their products from one country to another, which adds to the difficulty of pinpointing the source; the growing number of wildlife farms and ranches also confuses the issue.

The World Wide Fund for Nature estimates that illegal wildlife trade has increased by 25 per cent in the last five years. Similar to drug-traffickers in many ways, dealers can pick up an animal product (or even an animal) for next to nothing in its country of origin, and sell it at ridiculously high prices in the more affluent West. Unlike drug dealers, however, those who sell wildlife products are unlikely to get life imprisonment, and certainly aren't risking the death penalty!

THE SOLUTION

- Whether collecting souvenirs on your travels, or buying from a shop or dealer nearer home, avoid at all costs:

    O Ivory from elephants and from marine mammals such as whales, walruses, and narwhals, often carved into figurines, curios or jewellery. African elephants live in small herds of closely knit family groups, led by one or two older females. If (and it's a big 'if') they survive poaching, they can reach the age of seventy. The African Wildlife Foundation has estimated that 80,000 adult African elephants are killed every year for their tusks, and that another 10,000 youngsters die as a result (some are killed in the process of poaching, but most starve to death).

    O Tortoise-shell jewellery and combs, or leather, eggs, food products, and creams and cosmetics made with turtle flesh extract. Twenty thousand endangered sea turtles are slaughtered every year in Mexico, many as they are crawling back to sea, exhausted, after laying their eggs.

    O Rugs, pelts, hunting trophies, and articles such as handbags, compacts, coats, wallets, and key cases made from the skins or furs of wild cats, including jaguars, leopards, snow leopards and tigers, ocelots, margays, and small tiger cats. An American organisation called Earth

Island Institute reports that more than 90 per cent of Nepal's fur shop coats are made from protected species. It takes approximately four rare snow leopards to make a coat, or at least thirty 'common' leopard cats.

O Marine mammal products, such as whales' teeth decorated with etchings *(scrimshaw)* or made into figurines *(netsuke)*, curios, and jewellery, or the furs and skins of marine mammals: sealskin toys, purses, wallets, key cases, and clothing; sea otter furs and clothing; and polar bear hunting trophies, rugs, and clothing. Scientists estimate that at one time there may have been as many as 2 million blue whales, the largest animals ever to roam the planet. There are now fewer than 500. Geneticist Joseph Cummins predicts that polar bears could be extinct in fifteen years.

O Handbags and shoes made from reptile skins and leathers, particularly those from Latin America, the Caribbean, China, and Egypt. (Endangered species include black caiman, spectacled caiman, American crocodile, Orinoco crocodile from Latin America and the Caribbean, Philippine crocodile, Chinese alligator, and Nile crocodile.) The World Wide Fund for Nature's list of endangered and threatened animals includes 1,200 animal species, including at least forty-six varieties of turtle, twenty-two of crocodile, and twenty-four of snake.

O Wild birds' feathers, mounted birds, and skins; and all live birds, including macaws, originating in Australia, Brazil, Ecuador, Mexico, Paraguay, Venezuela, and a number of Caribbean countries.

• Though it is obviously vitally important to preserve our endangered wildlife, *all* animals feel pain, all have a will to live. Make a resolution, therefore, never to buy any souvenir you suspect has been made by causing animal suffering.

• CITES has put together a list of animals so close to extinction that it is illegal to trade in them, or in any products made from them. This list is continually being updated from the Swiss headquarters.

40

IS YOUR JOURNEY REALLY NECESSARY?

Too many walkers can wear out the environment just as
surely as a platoon of tanks.
JOHN ELKINGTON and JULIA HAILES,
The Green Consumer Guide

THE PROBLEM

We are all on the move, never still, always looking for
something new to try, still believing that just over the next hill
is where dreams come true. And wherever this restlessness
takes us – whether it's a drive down to the coast for the day,
skiing in winter, a three-month trip across India, or a winter
cruise around the Greek islands – we cause damage to our
environment, and do incredible harm to the animals who share
it with us.

Some Facts to Take with You

- At the moment tourism is the world's third largest industry;
  it is expected that, by the end of the decade, it will be the
  largest.
- Each year some 30 million British tourists set off for
  destinations around the world, encouraging local businessmen
  to build vast hotel complexes on remote beaches, increasing
  the discharge of sewage into once-pure seas – making it
  almost impossible to get away from noise, pollution and
  people.
- Though not intentionally, tourism is responsible for many of
  the threats that growing numbers of other-than-humans are
  now facing. For example, in Greece and Turkey, long-
  established breeding beaches for loggerhead turtles are now
  surrounded by hotels; the hatchlings, who should be drawn to
  the sea by moonlight on water, are being distracted by the

resorts' brighter lights and lured in the wrong direction with the result that when day comes they are either run over or die from dehydration. In Scotland, proposed ski slopes are threatening the habitats of the golden plover. A team of volunteers recently climbed Mount Everest specifically to clear the vast amounts of rubbish left by previous climbers, much of which was posing a threat to wildlife.

- More deliberate cruelties are also plentiful. Baby chimpanzees are used (illegally) by Spanish photographers as an enticement to have your photograph taken – an enticement that works especially well with the British, Dutch and Germans, all of whom seem to share a love of seeing animals dressed up in funny clothes. What we do not see is the way these babies are treated during their short lives (drugged, their teeth pulled, beaten – and killed after a couple of years when they become too big to handle). In Italy, lion cubs are often abused in much the same way. Though bull-fighting is undoubtedly popular with older Spaniards, the tourists it attracts help keep this barbaric 'entertainment' going. The debilitated and tormented animal in fact stands no chance against the 'brave' matadors; he has had Vaseline smeared into his eyes, his horns filed blunt, cotton stuffed up his nose to make breathing difficult. No wonder that 90 per cent of those tourists who attend never return.

- Wildlife is also becoming a tourist attraction in its own right – and to its disadvantage. As interest in animals grows we flock to see them. A continual stream of coaches through some of Kenya's game parks is turning the ground to dust and polluting the air. The grey whales of California are having to be protcted from over-eager sightseers. One nesting pair of ospreys in Scotland drew hundreds of people to stay at the nearby village, transforming a remote spot into a bustling centre.

- Not all wildlife 'holidays' are run with concern for animals. In India there was an outcry when it was reported that, in one game reserve, goats were being tied up near to where the coaches parked so that tourists could see the lions at kill.

- Even driving around the country can do untold harm to animals. Just look along the side of the road; fast cars are lethal weapons that take the lives of hedgehogs, foxes, badgers, rabbits, birds, frogs and toads. Butterflies and insects are splattered on the windows. One short journey can result in many deaths.

THE SOLUTION

- Think before you go anywhere! If your journey is a local one, consider walking, or going by bike. If you must drive, do so with a sharp eye open for animals and birds. And if you think you might have hit one, never just drive on; go back and check. Many animals who die on the roads have only been stunned by a first vehicle, but are then hit again simply because no one bothered to stop and assist them.

- When holidaying in Britain, move around with care. By all means explore some of the beautiful places we have (go walking, bird-watching, canoeing), but remember the famous adage, 'Take nothing but pictures, leave nothing but footprints, kill nothing but time.' There are also organised holidays for studying such things as herbalism or organic gardening (contact the National Centre for Alternative Technology, Machynlleth, Powys, Wales SY20 9AZ). Or consider a working holiday; the British Trust for Conservation Volunteers always need help (36 St Mary's Street, Wallingford, Oxon OX10 0EU). Help count birds, or assist with a survey of our coastline.

- If planning a holiday abroad, choose with care. A growing number of countries are now becoming aware that package tours are not necessarily the key to a prosperous future, and are building fewer hotels, siting these more carefully. Some travel firms are giving a percentage of the money you pay to societies such as the World Wide Fund for Nature; others are offering 'low-impact' holidays. A new organisation called Green Flag International is putting out a travel pack (price £5) which gives lots of help and down-to-earth advice; you will also receive a £5 voucher you can use against any holiday you may book with one of the nineteen tour operators and travel companies that are working with Green Flag.

- Many holidays abroad are ruined, for animal protectionists, not just by the distressing number of stray cats and dogs, but by the way in which they are treated. What makes it worse is the feeling of helplessness. In fact, there are many British organisations working on the Continent, some with local sanctuaries, and there may well be one where you were going. Check before you leave by ringing the National Canine Defence League on (071) 388 0137. If you are confronted with more organised cruelties – such as bull-fighting, Spanish fiestas, cock-fights – make it clear that you are not interested. When possible, encourage other visitors to boycott them too. If you are on a package tour, complain to the representative, and write to the company when you get back home. (In 1990 the Mayor of Tossa de Mar, on the Spanish Costa Brava, announced a ban on bull-fighting and fiestas involving animals, organising instead a four-day animal rights and 'green' festival in May. If you are going to Spain, do show your approval by visiting his village.)

- Do you really need to go on that safari? Wild animals need space, peace and freedom. By encouraging tourism to wild places you are encroaching on their already-restricted environment. You are also teaching them to hang around or beg for food rather than find their own, making them dependent (at the same time putting them in danger from foods that are unnatural for them – or from rubbish such as plastic bags!). You are changing their whole way of life and probably, most dangerous of all, you are de-fusing their natural wariness of human beings! There are some excellent wildlife videos now available. Why not save money and watch these instead?

RESOURCES

- *The Green Consumer Guide*, John Elkington and Julia Hailes (Gollancz 1988). Has a very useful and informative section on eco- and animal-friendly travelling.
- Green Flag International, P.O. Box 396, Linton, Cambridge CB1 6UL.
- *The International Vegetarian Travel Guide*, published by the Vegetarian Society (UK). By mail order from the Merchandise Department, VSUK, price £5.50 plus £1.50 p&p.

IT'S THE VEAL THING

You may love the pup-dog for his good humour, admire the fish for his face, feel like a brother to the noble horse, but no bird, beast or reptile can compare with the cow. You look into her eyes and she reads your troubles, sighs, and stops chewing her cud . . .

CHARLTON OGBURN, JR,
Animals' Voice Magazine, February 1989

I'm somewhat shy about the facts of being a carnivore. I don't like meat to look like animals. I prefer it in the form of sausages, hamburger and meat loaf, far removed from the living thing.

JOHN UPDIKE,
interview for the *New York Times* News Service, 1982

You have just dined, and however scrupulously the slaughterhouse is concealed in the graceful distance of miles, there is complicity.

RALPH WALDO EMERSON, *Fate*

As long as there are slaughterhouses there will be battlefields.

LEO TOLSTOY

THE PROBLEM

Although most people who really care about animals gave up eating veal long ago, many people are deluded that other bovines frolic in sunny, grass-filled meadows until they are 'humanely' killed for food. And milk is believed to have somehow been donated by mother cows anxious to share with human beings. This is not, however, the reality for the calf's mother and father.

• There are some 3 million 'milk machines' in Britain, dairy cows who are kept continually pregnant so that we can have their milk. Only a tiny minority of our dairy herds live a natural existence, the remainder being kept in 'factory' conditions, on slatted or concrete floors that cause their legs to weaken and buckle and their feet to become deformed. For months at a time they may be confined in such stalls, being milked where they stand. Growth hormones make their udders so heavy and swollen they sometimes drag along the ground, where teats get bruised, cut, and infected; the cow in peak lactation produces 35 litres of milk each day, more than ten times what her calf would need. These hormones can be passed on to humans through milk and meat, causing problems ranging from dysfunctional reproductive systems to premature sexual maturity.

- Instead of her usual lifespan of twenty-five years, the gentle dairy cow is allowed to live only three to five years. (Infertility or illness mean that 25 per cent of cows are prematurely 'culled' each year.) By her fourth lactation she will be close to her end, probably suffering with mastitis, gut and liver disorders. Most dairy cows become fast-food burgers.

- And what happens to her babies? Separated almost immediately after the birth, both the cow and her calf will suffer dreadful anguish, crying loudly. Female calves are either slaughtered immediately (to be used in foods like veal and ham pie) or raised to become milk machines like their mothers. Most male calves will be fattened quickly on a high protein diet (this may well be based on barley, which frequently leads to liver abscesses) and slaughtered before they are eighteen months old.

- All this suffering is so that human beings – the only species that drinks milk beyond infancy (and not even that of their own species!) – can have their 'liquid meat'.

- Calves bred for white veal are confined in narrow wooden crates, often chained by the neck, usually in darkness and without bedding, unable to turn, to lie down comfortably, to touch the animals chained up alongside them. They are fed a diet deficient in iron and fibre (milk-fed veal is just that!), suffer from anaemia and other illness, and are often too weak to walk when – after four months – they are hauled off for slaughter. Veal crates are now banned in Britain. However, Britain exported 30,000 calves overseas in 1989, the majority destined to live their short lives in foreign veal crates – and a large proportion of the veal on sale in butchers and restaurants in this country is imported, much of it from animals born here, which surely makes a mockery of our law.

Did You Know?

- It takes 2,500 to 6,000 gallons of water to produce a pound of meat, but just 25 gallons to produce a pound of wheat. Intensive farming is also responsible for a great deal of water pollution; the disposal of vast amounts of slurry is a continual problem, slurry lagoons bursting and overflowing into rivers and lakes, slurry applied to fields seeping through to pollute underground water levels from which our tap water is taken. The 200 million tonnes of excreta produced by factory-farmed animals each year has a pollution potential three times that of human excreta.
- Incidents of food-related diseases are rising faster than any other illnesses in the human population, the majority of these coming from meat and poultry. In Britain our cattle also suffer from BSE ('Mad Cow' disease), a horrifying nerve disease that has almost certainly been passed to them by feeding them the processed remains of sheep infected with the disease scrapie. Nobody knows for sure if this disease can be passed to humans, and because the incubation period is so long, no one will know for many years. We do know, however, that other meat-producing animals (such as pigs) can contract BSE, though most of them will have been slaughtered well before any symptoms might show.
- Sixty million people will starve to death this year, yet a vegetarian world could amply support several times the current human population. For the 'feed cost' of an 8-ounce steak, forty-five to fifty people could each have a full cup of cooked cereal grains. Twenty pure vegetarians can be fed on the amount of land needed to feed one person consuming a meat-based diet.
- About 80 per cent of the world's population lack the enzyme

lactase to digest lactose, the milk sugar. It is only a small minority of people, therefore, who consider it so essential to health. *Is* it essential? The most common death in the Britain is by heart disease which kills one in every three people, many prematurely. By eliminating meat, eggs – and dairy products too – from your diet (becoming a vegan), you reduce your risk of heart attack dramatically.

WHAT YOU CAN DO

- Join the growing ranks of vegans: stop consuming cows, and the milk meant for their young. Breast cancer rates are nearly four times higher for women who eat meat daily than for vegan women. Prostate cancer rates are more than three times higher for men who eat animal products than for vegan men. A study into osteoporosis in women between the ages of fifty and eighty-nine found that the vegetarians lost only half the bone mass lost by non-vegetarians.
- Make the transition to a diet free of meat and dairy products by using substitutes, all of which are better for you, and most of which are cheaper, than cow products. Here's how to substitute for:

  O *Meat*: In place of ground beef in shepherd's pie, spaghetti sauces, tacos, chillis, and lasagne filling, use 'textured vegetable protein' (say protein with the fat removed). There are a number of companies making these, and you might even find one being sold 'loose', thus saving money and trees. Other substitutes include ready-made tofu and tempeh burgers, available at most whole-food and healthfood stores.

  O *Milk*: Soy milk has become sophisticated, now offering you varieties that include unsweetened, sweetened (with sugar or concentrated fruit juice), organic, a creamier 'gold top', concentrated (good as a cream substitute), and flavoured to make a 'milk-shake' type drink. Names to look out for are Plamil, Granose, Provamel, Unisoy. Your local supermarket may well have its own brand. Soya milks are lower in fat than cow's milk, and are, of course, cholesterol free. They go well on cereal, in drinks, and can be used for cooking.

O *Ice cream*: As dairy products are the leading cause of food allergies in humans, and as people are abandoning dairy products for ethical reasons, a number of non-dairy frozen desserts have become available in a selection of delicious flavours. Soya yoghurts are also now easy to find and taste good.

O *Cheese*: Non-dairy soy cheese, such as Scheese, mimics the taste and consistency of dairy cheese, and can be eaten raw or cooked. Tofu can be used in vegan lasagnes and cheescake recipes, and nutritional yeast sprinkled on tofu, broccoli, cauliflower and popcorn provides a cheesy taste.

O Recognise meat for what it really is: the antibiotic and pesticide-laden corpse of a tortured animal. John Harvey Kellogg, MD, wrote, 'A dead cow or sheep lying in a pasture is recognised as carrion. The same sort of a carcass dressed and hung up in a butcher's stall passes as food!'

O Join the stamina-bolstered vegetarian world of Dave Scott, six-time Triathlon winner; Tony La Russa, Oakland Athletics baseball team manager; Edwin Moses, undefeated for eight years in 400-metre hurdles; Paavo Nurmi, winner of twenty world records in distance running, and nine Olympic medals; Estelle Gray and Cheryl Marek, world record holders for cross-country tandem cycling; and Ridgely Abele, winner of eight national championships in karate.

O Heed the words of Dr Neal Barnard, president of the Physicians Committee for Responsible Medicine: 'We are primates, and primates are all vegetarians with only rare meat consumption by certain species. All the protein, minerals, and vitamins the human body needs are easily obtained from plant sources. The taste for meats and other fatty foods is like a substance abuse to which we are addicted early in life. While we have been struggling – and failing – to cure heart disease and cancer, their primary causes are right under our noses, on the dinner table.'

42

SORTING GOOD TOYS FROM BAD

> How would you like a big giant to come up to you and put
> some drops in your eyes and you couldn't touch them and
> just because the giant wanted to do an experiment he
> made you die? I think that [toy companies] should find
> another way to do an experiment! What good will it do
> to put a drop into an animal's eye, and then the animal
> dies? Animals (especially dogs) can help people in many
> ways. But then if you kill them, how can they help people?
> MINDI THOMPSON, letter to PETA Kids, February 1990

> We must combat society's indoctrination that portrays
> animals as things without rights. We must make young
> people aware. It's surprising what they can do with the
> right information. They are our future.
> SANDY LARSON, in Karen and Michael Iacobbo's
> 'Sandy Larson: Humane Educator',
> *Animals' Agenda*, May 1990

THE PROBLEM

Unbelievably, some toy manufacturers still test their toys on
animals (and no, this doesn't mean a company lets dogs carry
toys around in their mouths or play with them!). For example,
in recent tests a toy gun that shoots capsules of paint was shot at
close range into the eyes of rabbits. Not only toys themselves,
but the materials that go into them are force-fed in huge
quantities to rabbits, guinea pigs and rats. Painful tests on
animals do nothing to protect young consumers, who risk injury
when using projectile-shooting toys. For this reason, several
cities in the USA, including Chicago and Milwaukee, are
considering legislation to ban toy guns that shoot projectiles.

Many games – though they may look innocent – are
reinforcing the message that other-than-humans are to be

mocked, feared or destroyed. A game called 'Mousetrap' encourages children to design and build their own crazy trap, another called 'Hairy Horrors' turns spiders into something to send shivers up young spines. Far worse, though, are the small selection of toys and novelty items that actually glamorise, trivialise, and even promote animal abuse. For example: 'Wacko the Cockroach', a big soft ball (that looks far more like a bumble bee!) that – when smashed with the rubber mallet that is also supplied – races around the floor squealing. Or 'Krushed Kitty', a plush half-cat toy to hang from the boot of a car or other 'kitty krushing' place.

THE SOLUTION

- Protest to any companies you know are still testing their toys on other-than-humans (and if you don't know but have doubts, write and ask them – the more letters they get the quicker they'll come to realise that this is an important issue for many people). Fisher-Price, one of the biggest suppliers of toys in Britain, refuse to commit themselves to a permanent ban on hurting and killing animals. Write and tell them what you think of their heel-dragging: Fisher-Price, P.O. Box 100, Peterlee, Co. Durham SR8 2RF.

- Complain to the managers of any local stores carrying toys and novelties that promote animal cruelty or denigrate other-than-human beings. Encourage friends and family to do the same.

- Remember that you can help shape a child's attitudes to animals: choose toys that are not only informative but actively promote compassion. If buying a cuddly toy animal, try to choose those made to look like the real thing (and not prettified to make it more endearing!). Never, of course, buy anything made from real fur or skin. There are an increasing number of good toys and games in the shops. Or check through the many catalogues put out by societies campaigning on behalf of animals and the environment (such as Greenpeace, the Royal Society for the Protection of Birds, the RSPCA, Oxfam and Traidcraft). The World Wide Fund for Wildlife, for example, sell a game for three—five-year-olds called 'Memory Game', which teaches them to name and group a selection of animals. It's also beautifully made.

43

(GET THE) CHICKEN OUT

I think that the battery hen is the most miserable creature
in the feathered world today.
LORD HOUGHTON OF SOWERBY,
speaking in the House of Lords,
2 February 1981

If a robin redbreast in a cage
Puts all heaven in a rage,
How feels heaven when
Dies the billionth battery hen?
SPIKE MILLIGAN, *Animals' Voices Magazine*,
February 1989

Suffering . . . no matter how multiplied . . . is always
individual.
ANNE MORROW LINDBERG

THE PROBLEM

If you ever have the opportunity to get to know individual
chickens, you will find, as you do with dogs, cats, and people,
that some are shy, some brave, some more affectionate or
outgoing than others. Each is a sensitive, feeling individual with
his or her own distinct personality. Chickens make delightful,
curious, and dear companions. Unfortunately, chickens are
among the most maltreated and oppressed of all animals in
Britain today. Every year, producers for whom profits override
common decency subject some 38 million laying hens and 600
million broiler chickens to misery that defies description –
conditions that are also, in the opinion of Chickens' Lib and
others, breaking the law.

Did You Know?

• Nowadays chickens are genetically engineered and bred
  specifically for egg-laying or for meat. Since only female

chickens lay eggs, each year 50 million male chicks, only a day old, are gassed with carbon dioxide (though often they survive and are noticed moving about amongst dead birds bought as feed for other animals). In the USA baby chicks are usually macerated.

- Many battery farmers debeak their hens to discourage them from pecking each other, a habit caused by the stress, boredom and misery of their short lives. This painful mutilation is usually carried out on very young chicks using a searing wire that, because time is money to workers, sometimes takes part of their little tongues or faces, too.

- They are then placed in 18-inch by 20-inch wire battery cages with slanted wire floors to live with four other hens in spaces so jam-packed that they can't even stretch a wing. (New European Community regulations have imposed a legal minimum area of floor space that is in fact no larger than it has been in recent years!) Excrement from cages stacked above them splatters hens below. Raw sores take the place of feathers. Feet designed to walk on the earth become deformed from the wire, legs become crippled, wings atrophy, and bones become so brittle that they can and often do snap.

- A chicken can live for five to ten years, but factory-farmed hens are mostly 'used up' in eighteen months, then pulled from their cages and stuffed into crates for a terrifying and probably long ride to the slaughterhouse (and there is no legal limit on the time poultry can spend in transit). There, their feet attached to a conveyor belt, flapping to right themselves, they should, by law, be rendered unconscious by an electric stunner before their necks are cut. However, because the force of the shock may shatter their brittle bones (bone splinters in the meat are not a plus!), the voltage is frequently reduced, so that the hens may be fully conscious even when dumped into the scalding tanks. Intensively reared broiler (or table) chickens are slaughtered at just seven weeks of age. They will have baby-blue eyes and a high-pitched 'cheep'.

- Turkeys, once reared just for the Christmas market, are a fast-growing 'industry'; over 33 million were slaughtered in

1988. (Bernard Matthews accounts for 9 million of them – at least seventeen genetically different species including a stunted mini-bird – from which he produces burgers, mince, drumstick-shaped chopped turkey, and sausages. His advertising key-word 'bootiful' certainly doesn't apply to the lives of the birds – nor to the condition of nearby rivers which he has been charged with polluting twenty-seven times!) More closely related to the pheasant and partridge than chickens, turkeys suffer even more from being closely confined in factory farm conditions. Their natural frustration makes them prone to resort to cannibalism; hence they are often debeaked a second time, or reared in near-darkness. Because they are now also bred to grow unnaturally heavy – they may weigh as much as a nine-year-old child – around 80 per cent of males suffer from irreversible diseases of the hip joints. Imagine how they must suffer when held upside down in shackles, fully conscious, for six minutes or longer.

WHAT YOU CAN DO

- Avoid all poultry flesh and 'products', including eggs. (You'll be being kind, and safeguarding your health too.)
- When recipes call for eggs, simply leave the eggs out, replace them with soya flour or silken tofu, or use an egg substitute (there are now a couple on the market which you should be able to find at your local wholefood shop). Bananas can be used as a 'binder' in sweet recipes (half a banana equals the holding power of one egg).
- If you crave the taste and texture of chicken, try 'chicken-style Quorn in myco-protein pieces'. At the moment it comes ready made up in dishes such as pies and stir-fries. Some wheat-gluten dishes have a very similar texture.
- Tell your family and friends the facts about chickens and eggs and help them to stop eating them. Point out, too, that 80 per cent or more of oven-ready chickens are now contaminated with salmonella, and up to 60 per cent may have listeria. Suggest to local restaurants that they add more vegan dishes to their menus; then eat there (preferably with friends) to show their efforts are not wasted. Do the same in your work, school or college cafeteria.

- Alert others by writing letters to editors to protest the cruel treatment of chickens and turkeys in this country, and the health risks of eating their meat.
- Ask your grocer to have a vegetarian line at the store, so you won't have to put your groceries on a conveyor belt full of blood and salmonella leaked from packs of red meat and chicken.
- Be aware that 'free-range' egg-producers also kill the male hatchlings, and few let 'spent' hens retire in their old age.
- Broaden your eating horizons both in ethnic restaurants that specialise in savoury animal-free dishes, and with new recipes in your own kitchen.
- At Christmas, have printed (or copied) some suggested recipes to replace turkey and hand them out with a leaflet on how turkeys are raised. Chickens' Lib and Compassion in World Farming should be able to supply the leaflets. Wish your friends a 'cruelty-free holiday season'.
- Join up with one of the many organisations campaigning for a better deal for poultry; write to your MP and Euro MP, get petitions signed, organise demos to take place outside factory farms. Don't give up!

RESOURCES
- Chickens' Lib, P.O. Box 2, Holmfirth, Huddersfield, Yorkshire HD7 1QT.
- Compassion in World Farming, 20 Lavant Street, Petersfield, Hampshire GU32 3EW.
- The Vegetarian Society (UK) Ltd., Parkdale, Dunham Road, Altrincham, Cheshire WA14 4QG.

44

GIFT TABOOS AND GIFT 'TO-DO'S'

> So my Christmas present was a fur coat. I froze. How could I show gratitude or pleasure when all I could think of was the ugly way in which those twenty or so foxes must have lost their lives?
>
> MARYBETH TODD

BACKGROUND

When shopping for humans, give other-than-humans a gift, too – by checking your list to make sure your choices aren't naughty, but nice to all animals! By exercising your consumer clout, you can refuse to help cruel businesses continue to profit from animal suffering. You'll also get a feeling of satisfaction knowing that every pound you spend on products from animal-friendly companies helps them grow and expand. Your gifts will also send a positive message to your friends and family.

TABOOS

- You wouldn't want your friends to look like prehistoric cave-dwellers, would you? So steer clear of fur, leather, wool, down, silk, and animal skins when you are gift shopping. With all the humane alternatives available, there's no excuse for the ruthless slaughter of animals.
- If cosmetics or perfume are on a friend's wish-list, hit the cosmetics giants still testing on animals where it counts: at the cosmetics counter. Don't buy – and tell the vendors and producers why not – products made by companies still testing on other-than-human beings, like Guerlain (which also uses pig fat in its processing!), Calvin Klein and Lancôme. Instead, choose Christian Dior's 'Dior', Elizabeth Taylor's 'Passion' (but beware – some bottles come in a mink pouch), Benetton's 'Colours', and perfume by Yardley of London.

- Don't succumb to the temptation to give an animal as a gift. Such a gift is only appropriate if you are absolutely certain that the recipient has met and wants this particular companion animal (not one who just looks similar or has the same colouring); has the time and physical and financial ability to care for him or her properly (veterinary care is expensive); and understands and can accept the enormous responsibility and lifelong commitment to the animal. Then, get the animal from a shelter, not a 'pet' shop or breeder.

TO-DO'S

- For those who love to cook, a year's subscription to the *Vegan* (from the Vegan Society, 7 Battle Road, St Leonards-on-Sea, East Sussex TN37 7AA; price £6) is four gifts in one. Or how about six issues of the *Vegetarian* (from the Vegetarian Society (UK), Parkdale, Dunham Road, Altrincham, Cheshire WA14 4QG; price £8.50)? Both magazines contain not just enticing recipes but lots of informative articles. There are also dozens of vegetarian cookbooks which are sure to get tastebuds tingling; or give her/him a chance to get out of the kitchen with an invitation to dine at a good vegetarian restaurant.

- Introduce others to cruelty-free living with a decorative basket full of bath, hair and other personal-care products available from the Body Shop. If that sounds too expensive, choose just a single item (they'll gift wrap it for you). Choose from oodles of exotic products that include passion fruit cleansing gel, Japanese washing grains, carrot sun oil, plus a range of specially-for-men products. Culpeper also offers a wide selection of delicious-sounding products, all made without cruelty to animals. Look for scented soap leaves, birth sign sachets of pot pourri, 1920s style apothecary jars. Or buy a gift voucher; your friends will be overwhelmed by the hundreds of wonderful products to choose from! They'll want to spend hours sniffing at the Body Shop's perfume bar where they can mix fabulous scents together to create their own one-of-a-kind signature fragrance. Write to the Body Shop at Hawthorn Road, Littlehampton, West Sussex BN17 7LR; and to Culpeper Ltd, Hadstock Road, Linton,

Cambridge CB1 6NJ for your nearest shops and product lists (Culpeper also do mail order).

- Most animal rights societies have gift catalogues, the profits from sales going directly to help them in their work. Ideas might include a threatened forest jigsaw (World Wide Fund for Nature) or a cassette of eerily beautiful whale songs (Whale and Dolphin Conservation Society). Records on the All Change label are great to listen to; they also always contain a message about animals (like the new 'Chimp Rap'!). Details from the Mobile Animal Shop (P.O. Box 10, Ryde, Isle of Wight PO33 1JX), who also have a selection of gift ideas including *The Celebrity Vegetarian Cookbook* (in which fifty-five celebrities tell you what they like to eat).

- A birdbath or feeder, or a squirrel feeder or nesting box, will invite bushy-tailed or winged acrobats whose antics are sure to provide endless amusement. Get one from your local pet shop, nursery garden, or the Royal Society for the Protection of Birds (RSPB).

- Make up a vegetarian gift basket – or have your local wholefood store make one up for you. Load it with mushroom pâté, wild rice pilaf, spicy bean dip, tahini, exotic dried fruits, and vegan chocolates.

- Give a cotton kimono, cotton espadrilles, or a cotton-covered, cedar-chip dog bed.

- Give Findhorn Foundation 'Trees for Life' calendars or diaries (from The Park, Forres IV36 0TZ, Scotland), which have exquisite photographs. (Your money will be used to help preserve Scotland's Caledonian Forest, which has been reduced to 1 per cent of its original extent.) Check other environmental and animal rights societies too – especially for all those Christmas cards.

- Give flower or vegetable seeds, a window box, a sprouting kit, a lilac bush, a herb garden, an organic vegetable gardening magazine subscription, or copies of Helen and Scott Nearing's books *Living the Good Life* and *Continuing the Good Life*.

45

LOBSTER TALES

Poor animals! How jealously they guard their pathetic bodies . . . that which to us is merely an evening's meal, but to them is life itself.

T. CASEY BRENNAN

They really are very interesting little creatures. And to look into those eyes and to know that's a hundred million years of history – it's incredible.

CAM MACQUEEN, PETA lobster liberator

The Vice President identifies with any creature heading for hot water.

Press secretary to US vice-president DAN QUAYLE (commenting on Mr Quayle's decision to spare the life of a thirty-year-old, 13-pound lobster presented to him in March 1990)

THE PROBLEM

What if grocery stores kept live dogs (or even commonly consumed cows) crammed in filthy glass containers with their legs taped together, and what if accompanying recipes suggested dropping the fully-conscious animals into a pot of boiling water? People would be outraged. But swap the mammalian victims for those with claws and antennae, and who cries of 'injustice!'?

Crustacean Revelation

● Lobsters are fascinating. They have a long childhood and an awkward adolescence. They use complicated signals to explore and establish social relationships with others. Their communications are direct and sophisticated. They flirt. Their pregnancies last nine months. Some are right-handed, some left-handed. They've even been seen walking hand-in-hand! Some can live to be more than 150 years old, though few (1 per cent) survive the world's most devastating predator – the species with whom lobsters share so many traits – the human being.

- Like us, lobsters are vertebrates who feel pain; when they are tossed into scalding water, their claws scrape the sides of the pot as they struggle to get out. Their frantic and fruitless efforts have caused more than a kitchenful of cooks pangs of guilt.

- Crustaceans are sensitive creatures who possess a will to live and who struggle as best they can against death. Knowing lobsters and crabs feel pain, we shouldn't allow prejudice to dictate to our palates and consciences.

- As few lobsters are caught around our coasts, and as yet there are no lobster farms in Britain, most of those on sale in restaurants and shops will have been imported, crammed together in packing cases piled one on top of the other, unable to move for journeys that could last days. A Canadian exporter is reported to be experimenting with a new technique that involves packing each lobster in a plastic tube, and then reducing its body temperature; under such conditions, he believes, a lobster will go into a torpor and will therefore stay fresh for long periods.

- 'University of Maine researchers say that "ghost traps" (traps lost on the sea or bay floor) are keeping many lobsters trapped for months and sometimes even years. Lobsters can survive indefinitely in the lost and abandoned traps because enough food passes through to keep them alive. A new law requires that all wire lobster traps be equipped with a biodegradable escape panel that opens after a period of time' (*Animals' Voice Magazine*, Vol. 6, No. 2).

- Oysters, once a luxury food, are now being factory farmed in order to provide a plentiful, cheap supply for what is hoped will be a growing demand. These oysters will not be used for making pearls; their destiny is to be consumed while still young and tender. Traditionally oysters are eaten raw.

WHAT YOU CAN DO
- Eliminate lobsters, crabs, and other sea animals from your diet. There are plenty of reasons not to eat them, including

bacterial contamination and seafood poisoning (which even the government has warned against). Your body, designed to digest a flesh-free diet, will thank you for avoiding an unnecessary strain.

- In restaurants with live lobster tanks, voice your objection and follow up with a letter of complaint. Point out that these nocturnal creatures deserve better than to exist on display in crowded tanks twenty-four hours a day. Let the owner or manager know that you look forward to eating there again only when the tank has been removed, and that you will be encouraging your friends, family, and co-workers to boycott as well.

- Write letters of complaint to supermarkets and stores that sell live lobsters. Tell them exactly why you object.

46

THE SHOW MUST *NOT* GO ON

The wild, cruel beast is not behind the bars of the cage. He is in front of it.

AXEL MUNTHE

THE PROBLEM

Circuses that feature animals may draw cheers from the audience but they are no fun for the animals. Show sponsors force the animals to 'give up' their natural lives, swapping the forests and jungles for a miserable existence in travel trailers that they call 'beast wagons'. The animals are trained to perform repetitive, puzzling (to them), grossly uncomfortable, dangerous, and frightening acts, such as standing on their heads or jumping through hoops of fire (instinctively feared by most animals).

- In circuses, bears are kept in neck chains and muzzles, elephants stay shackled by one front and one back leg for the greater part of twenty-four hours, and big cats have their claws removed. Most of them leave their cages for only an hour or two each day, rarely see sunlight, feel the ground, or experience the touch or companionship of another animal.
- Circus 'giants' such as Gerry Cottle and Chipperfield insist that good trainers never use violence and always 'encourage' animals to learn their feats with kindness and rewards. Most animal behaviourists doubt that wild animals can be taught to do things so unnatural, uncomfortable and alien to them without being forced to. Undercover investigators confirm widespread use of the whip, the hook, and the electric prod.
- The circus industry also points out that shows with animals are of educational benefit to children, and that it may be one of the few chances they get to see exotic animals close up. But what exactly do these children learn? That animals are dumb creatures for us to use as we wish? That they are ridiculous buffoons to be laughed at? That elephants are good dancers and that tigers like riding in cars?
- As circuses prefer to be based near town or city centres, it has long been traditional for them to set up on council land. However, due to the growing number of people who object to their abuse of animals, some 130 local authorities are now resolved not to let sites to circuses which contain animal acts.

WHAT YOU CAN DO
- Boycott all circuses that contain animal acts.
- If yours is one of the councils that still allow circuses with animal acts on their land, talk to your local councillor or MP. Explain why you think this should be stopped. Get others to sign a petition; write letters to local papers and ring in to a chat show on local radio.
- Should you be successful, the circus proprietors may still be able to perform somewhere locally by persuading a private

landowner to let them use his or her land. If this happens, try approaching the landowner and putting your case.

• Make every effort to ensure that as few people as possible go to any circus that does set up in your area. Again, write to newspapers and make sure you have your say on the radio. When you see a poster for the circus in a shop window, go in and ask the owner if s/he realises just how much circus animals suffer. Take in leaflets, or copies of the many articles that have been written recently exposing what really goes on behind the scenes. If s/he still won't take down the poster, suggest that yours is at least put up alongside it, to give the other side. (Do remember though that many shopkeepers are 'paid' for displaying the poster with free ring-side seats for themselves and family.)

• If the show is booked in spite of your efforts, be on the scene with picket signs and leaflets. Dressed in a clown, cowboy or other appropriate costume and with a friendly smile, you're sure to reach many people. Get some like-minded friends to join you.

• Many of the worst circuses are those found touring the Continent. One of the biggest, the Moscow State Circus, uses a variety of animal acts, some of their performances being on ice (though few of these animals acts come with the circus to Britain). If any overseas circus comes to your town, check first that it contains no animal acts – then go along and enjoy it. A circus can be an amusing, spellbinding, highly entertaining experience; support all those that have not just the skills but the true circus spirit without needing to abuse and degrade innocent animals in order to bring in the crowds.

• Educate the group that animal acts try to appeal to most: children. The majority of children have a natural affinity for *all* living things and are upset when (*if*) they learn about cruelty to animals. Take them to see a circus whose entertainment value comes from amusing and unusual human performances rather than pathetic other-than-human acts. Non-animal circuses include Ra Ra Zoo with acrobats, jugglers and trapeze artists, the Cirque du Soleil (a miracle of choreography and costumery), Circus Burlesque, which is unusual in that it tells a story, and Zippo's family circus (the only animal act in a recent performance was a daring human pantomime 'gorilla' on a tightrope!).

RESOURCES

For leaflets, information and support:

- Captive Animals' Protection Society, 36 Braemore Court, Kingsway, Hove, East Sussex BN3 4FG.
- RSPCA, The Causeway, Horsham, West Sussex RH12 1HG.
- Animal Aid, 7 Castle Street, Tonbridge, Kent TN9 1BH.

47

TIME OUT: CHOOSE ANIMAL RIGHTS, NOT ANIMAL 'SIGHTS'

> For what do the good people see who go to the gardens
> on a half-holiday afternoon to poke their umbrellas at a
> blinking eagle-owl, or to throw dog-biscuits down the
> expansive throat of a hippopotamus? Not wild beasts or
> birds certainly, for there never have been or can be such
> in the best of all possible menageries, but merely the
> outer semblances and *simulacra* of the denizens of forest
> and prairie — poor spiritless remnants of what were
> formerly wild animals.
>
> HENRY S. SALT, *Animals' Rights*

> The thinking [person] must oppose all cruel customs no
> matter how deeply rooted in tradition and surrounded by
> a halo. When we have a choice, we must avoid bringing
> torment and injury into the life of another . . .
>
> ALBERT SCHWEITZER

THE PROBLEM

Within the tourism and entertainment industries, it's a well-known fact that there has been Big Money in animals. Britain now has some 230 zoos/safari parks displaying thousands of animals, the majority living under conditions that are at best boring and restrictive, at worst not unlike the battery cages in which many factory-farmed animals are crammed.

- The Zoo Licensing Act of 1981 lays down only minimum standards of care and welfare for animals in captivity, and even these are frequently flouted, especially by the smaller establishments. Animals who, under natural conditions, would range many miles each day, are kept in cages barely two or three times their length. The ground is concrete for ease of cleaning; there are no trees, plants, no running water. Animals who come from the Arctic (like polar bears) and the desert (like camels) are all expected to adapt to the British climate, despite the fact that their bodies are completely wrong for our environment. Gorillas who, in the wild, live in family groups, find themselves alone in a cage. Other primates are often overcrowded, with aggression and other neurotic behaviour a direct result. Neurotic behaviour is the trademark of most zoos, with boredom being inevitable. In fact, many of the animals are barely alive – as a look into their eyes will tell anyone with a degree of sensitivity. Some zoos have tried to re-design living areas to provide some stimulation, but how can a cage ever compare with a jungle, mountains or woodland? The reality is that when a zoo announces 'improvements' it is most likely to mean importing an exotic and preferably 'endangered' species from the other side of the world, putting in some new flowerbeds, and opening a couple more hamburger stands.

- Safari parks, a more recent idea for exploiting animals, sometimes offer them a slightly better deal. Though most of them still have a large number of caged animals, the main attraction is usually a series of open areas in which prides of lions might live, or monkeys, and through which the visitor drives, choking the animals with fumes and discarded rubbish, but at least allowing them freedom of movement, and soil beneath their feet.

- For many years now campaigns to improve and even close down certain zoos have at least meant lower numbers at the gates, though the advantage to the animals of this reduction is, in the short term, dubious, as witness the situation at London Zoo.

- Despite conditions in zoos, some animals still breed very efficiently, which creates another problem. Various techniques are used to control this, such as hormonal implants for female tigers (tigers are notoriously good at reproducing). Still, though, there are inevitably too many animals for limited space and finances, which means some have to be 'culled'. A more sinister way in which certain zoos deal with this excess is to sell them to vivisection laboratories. On the same grounds as London Zoo can be found the Institute of Zoology, where a number of different species of animals passed on from the zoo are used in experiments. Others are sent from zoos such as Whipsnade. Born in captivity, having no concept of what their lives could and should have been, these wild animals end up being no more than disposable tools for a researcher.

- Though horse-racing is a highly popular spectator sport, it is also one that involves a good deal of cruelty. It was recently reported that 2 out of 3 thoroughbred racehorses suffer sprains each year, and 175 die during races. In the once-yearly Grand National alone some twenty horses have died, most of them at the particularly treacherous Becher's Brook jump; an outcry resulted in this being slightly adjusted, but it is still very dangerous to horses. Certainly it is natural and no doubt pleasurable for horses to run, but the habit of whipping them so that they continue even when exhausted must surely count as cruelty? The game of polo, during which horses are forced to change direction suddenly and frequently, can also result in severe pain to the animals, and sometimes major injury.

- Greyhounds, with their love of running (and their ability to reach speeds of forty miles per hour), look not just spectacular, but as though they are enjoying themselves on the track; unlike horses, they have no one forcing them beyond their capabilities. However, once their running life is over they become a problem. Certainly winning dogs may be put to stud, or allowed a comfortable retirement by fond owners. The majority, however, are unwanted. Many end up in shelters where they may stay, or be 'put down'. Their years spent chasing a small metal animal round a track make them difficult to re-home, people fearing they might be vicious (and would certainly not be popular with the family cat). An increasing number, it has emerged, are sent to vivisection laboratories.

- Although 'entertainments' such as cock-fighting, dog-fighting and badger-baiting are against the law, they are on the increase. Cock-fights and dog-fights are usually held in the country or in warehouses away from residential areas, and attended by those who are 'in the know', a good deal of money often changing hands after the fight. Death is inevitable for at least one of the unwitting participants, if not both. Less sinister sounding – and often popular with children – are such things as frog- and ferret-racing. Even these, however, involve the capture of wild other-than-humans who are transported somewhere they would sooner not be, then frightened and confused by noise, crowds and lights.

WHAT YOU CAN DO

- Boycott zoos and safari parks. (If you somehow get dragged to one, use the opportunity to take careful note of how it is run, what conditions the animals are in, and so on. If anything bothers you, take a note and send details to Zoo Check, the society campaigning for the improvement of and eventual phasing out of zoos.)
- As an alternative, visit one of John Aspinall's two zoo parks in Kent (listed below), which are really 'conservation' parks. Between them they have over 350 acres of land devoted to making animals as comfortable (and giving them as much privacy) as possible. Most of the animals are rare and endangered species who, it is hoped, might go back into the wild at some time. These include a gorilla colony, Sumatran rhinos, the only breeding herd of African elephants in Britain, and rare Przewalski horses (some of whom are just about to be set free in China). John Aspinall also runs a gorilla orphanage in the Congo; babies are nursed back to health then taught how to look after themselves.
- Is there a particular animal you want to study more closely? Rent or buy a video. There are now many companies offering a wide range of excellent films on all sorts of animals, most of them shot in the animals' natural environment, and showing aspects of the 'star's' true character and lifestyle that you would never see at a zoo.
- Don't pay to watch horses or dogs racing. You'll be supporting those who consider animals nothing more than a way of making money, not living beings with interests and rights.

- Dog-fighting, cock-fighting and badger-baiting are all illegal. Anyone who organises or participates in them can be fined and even sent to prison. If you are told about a forthcoming fight, or overhear something in a country pub, take a careful note of time and place and then inform the police. Do not decide to go along and take the law into your own hands; blood sports such as these do not bring out the best in the audience and you may well be letting yourself in for far more than you can handle!

RESOURCES
- Zoo Check, Cherry Tree Cottage, Coldharbour, Dorking, Surrey RH5 6HA; tel. (0306) 712091. Become a member and you will receive regular newsletters telling you what's happening in zoos around the world. Incorporates Elefriends and Junior Elefriends.
- Howletts Zoo Park, Bekesbourne, near Canterbury, Kent CT4 5EL; tel. (0227) 721286.
- Port Lympne Zoo Park, Lympne, near Hythe, Kent CT21 4PD; tel. (0303) 264646.

48

ADVERTISING ACTION

Let us dare to read, think, speak and write.
JOHN ADAMS, second president of the United States

THE PROBLEM
Given the British passion for animals, it isn't surprising that the advertisers use them so frequently in order to catch our attention. As we relax in front of the television set, or flick through a magazine, we see other-than-humans galore, all

types, all shapes and sizes, from elephants to mice, tigers to ginger toms. Our first reaction is usually 'how sweet' or 'how funny'. But maybe we should take a second look, think a little about how those animals were made to do the things they do – and possibly even more important – what effect their use in this way has on our attitude to animals in general.

- The Independent Television Commission (ITC) point out that many of the complaints they check out about television commercials featuring animals are, in fact, the results of highly advanced filming techniques. The gold and silver 'seals' were not painted; the colour was superimposed on the film. The cow in the rocking boat was actually a shot of a cow and a shot of a boat combined. The spinning dog, so determined to catch his tail, only spun round a couple of times; the film was then repeated. Use of such techniques is not only kinder to animals, but easier for film crews!
- There are, however, different kinds of abuse. The more obvious kind is when animals are hit, tripped, or even spun in a washing machine. But abuse can also be as subtle as forcing a cat to stay awake for hours in order to be able to sleep 'on cue', or yanking (repeatedly) on a parrot's tail to make him or her fall off a perch. The making of the award-winning commercial that featured a bulldog, a cat and a mouse in front of a fire must have been terrifying for the mouse, with his/her instinctive fear of cats, (if not for the cat too). There is also the fact that studios are usually hot, busy, noisy places, and that a thirty-second commercial can take a whole day or even longer to shoot. For any animal such conditions will be at best tiring and stressful; for some they will be torture.
- Because most of us watch so much television these days, our attitudes to many things are formed (almost without us noticing) by what we see. Many commercials simply feature animals as beautiful to watch, and though their links with the product may be tenuous, they can also give pleasure: the black horse or the huge pack of dogs racing across the hills, the tiger bounding across a beach (all of them having been trained to perform, of course – but hopefully enjoying the run). But what about the PG Tips chimpanzees, dressed to

look almost human, forced to 'say' the most ridiculous things? Or the orangutan with the umbrella, waiting in the rain to hitch a lift? Primates seem to be especially popular with advertisers intent on raising a laugh, yet they are beautiful and intelligent animals who deserve to be depicted with dignity, not as lesser (or inadequate quasi-) humans.

• Even cartoon animals can be used in ways that mislead. Chickens in a flap, feathers flying, knowing they are about to be eaten, are *not* funny. They mask the reality of what happens to real, live animals before they become something people buy pre-packed from a supermarket freezer, making murder not just acceptable but also humorous.

THE SOLUTION

We don't have to sit back passively – we can let advertisers know we want them to write animals out of their scripts, and that dancing cows and elephants balancing on one leg turn us away from, rather than towards the products they want us to buy.

• Keep a stack of blank, pre-stamped postcards by your television viewing chair. Whenever you see any animal doing something awkward, confusing, dangerous or demeaning – or a wild animal doing anything – write a polite 'opinion note' to the product manufacturer. Or write to the ITC, who have just drawn up a new Code of Practice which insists that no pain or distress is caused to an animal in the making of a commercial, and that nothing must be shown that might encourage cruelty or irresponsible behaviour towards animals; trivialisation is also discouraged. So if what you've just seen contravenes this code, they should object on your behalf. They will, in any case, pass on complaints to the manufacturers concerned, who will probably get back to you. Don't forget that – unlike producers of films, who may shock and distress you as part of the 'entertainment' they offer – advertisers need you to like and approve what they are doing. Their profits depend on it!

• It wouldn't do any harm to drop a line to your local television company as well (the one that ran the commercial) – they won't like to think they might lose viewers. Find their address in the *Yellow Pages* (look under 'Broadcasting Organisations').

- Advertisements that offend in magazines and newspapers should be reported to the Advertising Standards Authority (ASA), whose code is based on the four concepts: legal, decent, honest and truthful. If it causes offence it isn't decent!
- Take the postpaid subscription cards out of magazines that accept advertisements in which animals appear to be demeaned or abused, or that feature items made from fur, put your comments on them and pop them in the post.
- Officially the RSPCA is responsible for ensuring animals do not suffer during the preparation of either television commercials or press advertisments. You can always contact them if you have any doubts at all about anything you see, and providing there is just cause for your concern they will follow up your complaint.
- If you work for an advertising agency, educate your colleagues. Implement a policy like those of Ads Unlimited in New York, and Chase, Pickett, and Putscher Associates in Illinois, banning the use of animals by your agency – or try to get such a policy adopted. Point out that creative advertising is great, but compassionate creativity is greater!
- Type short, one- or two-paragraph letters to the editors of magazines that run ads that are detrimental to animals in any way. Also, write to producers of shows in which characters wear fur or in other ways demean or injure animals (see below).

Sample Notes

To the Editor:
I am very distressed to see [company name] using tigers to sell deodorant in your magazine. Tigers belong in the jungle, not in the studio. Animals used in advertisements are all too often abused in training, shipment, acquisition, and even disposal.

Until these advertisements are halted, I will not buy from [company name]. Animals are individuals with interests of their own, not merchandising tools. Please refuse to run ads like this.

Dear Producer,
I love [programme title] and was so sorry to see [its star] in what
appeared to be a lynx coat [day of the week]. [Star's character]
is surely not supposed to be so shallow and uncaring as to
patronise the slaughter of these magnificent cats. The other
characters' failure to criticise the coat as less than glamorous
seems out of touch with current public opinion against cruelty
to animals in the fur trade.

Your response would be appreciated.

RESOURCES
- Independent Television Commission (ITC), 70 Brompton
  Road, London SW3 1EY.
- Advertising Standards Authority (ASA), Brook House,
  Torrington Place, London WC1E 7HN.
- RSPCA, The Causeway, Horsham, West Sussex, RH12
  1HG.

49

DONATION DO'S AND DON'TS

> Charity is indivisible. If a man resents practical sympathy
> being bestowed on animals on the ground that all ought
> to be reserved for the species to which he himself
> happens to belong he must have a mind the size of a pin's
> head.
>
> C.W. HUME, *The Status of Animals*

BACKGROUND
Private philanthropy is a vital component of our society; it
bears much of the weight of coping with vast social and health

problems, pulling up the slack for a government increasingly unwilling to fund desperately needed services. Charity organisations and foundations that provide voices for the voiceless and succour for the needy require our support, but we must watch where donations go, no matter how prestigious the organisation.

BE INFORMED

● In 1989 the Cancer Research Campaign, one of the largest research charities in Britain, directed just 1.5 per cent of its vast expenditure to cancer education (yet at least 80 per cent of cancers are known to have environmental causes and are, in principle anyway, preventable). Much of the remaining money went on projects that have, to date, included injecting and implanting cancer cells into the eyes, brains, paws and abdomens of thousands of animals.

● Since 1945 more than 600,000 compounds have been tested on animals in the search for new anti-cancer drugs. Yet different species of animals react differently to chemicals. It has been suggested that conflicting animal results have not only failed to provide a cure for cancer, but have actually delayed and hampered advancement.

● The British Heart Foundation has not only spent millions of pounds on developing transplantation surgery, but has sacrificed the lives of some half a million animals in the UK this century for the same cause. Emphasis recently has been on the development of an artificial heart. In 1981 publicity was given to the miserable existence of a calf whose heart was removed at the age of three months and replaced with a mechanical pump. Attempts to replace the human heart with a mechanical one have been dismal failures, yet research continues. Transplants will never be able to make even a dent in the toll of deaths from heart disease. The major risk factors are well known and coronary heart disease is largely preventable. Yet still it remains the leading cause of death in Britain.

● It isn't only charities associated with medical research who abuse animals. Both the National Trust and the Woodland

Trust (in certain areas) allow fox- and stag-hunting on their land. Although money donated to these trusts is without doubt helping other species by protecting designated areas of land from development, don't foxes and stags also deserve protection? When asked for donations, point out the contradiction. Say you'll be happy to give once this has been ironed out. Or better still, go ahead and join so that you'll be entitled to have your say whenever the issue of hunting on trust land comes up – and make sure it comes up often!

- Some of the land owned by the Church is also used for fox-and stag-hunting. A subject worth bringing up with your vicar or priest?

- Ask exactly what your money will fund. If it includes experiments on animals, write 'I will resume contributions when you discontinue animal experiments' on the contribution form – and return it *without* a donation. If you feel you must support a particular medical charity, specify that your money is not to be used for research on animals – and ask for confirmation to that effect.

- Ask to review an annual report. Look beyond self-promotion for evidence of *tangible* programmes and gauges of success, such as numbers of indigent patients treated, numbers of wheelchairs, walkers, or hearing aids distributed, numbers of acres preserved, numbers of books or films donated to schools, or numbers of animals sterilised.

- Tell pro-hunting charities that you respect the 'life' in 'wildlife', and that the environment 'belongs' to other-than-human beings, too.

- Charities who raise funds by raffling fur or other items taken from animals, or who sponsor exploitative events such as horse-racing or circuses with animals, need to know why that makes you a *former* donor.

- Remember that your local shelters (for homeless beings of any species), hospices, and other direct-care facilities need your help – both hands-on and financial.

RESOURCE

- *Faith, Hope and Charity?* is a booklet by Dr Gill Langley, Ph.D. (available from the British Union for the Abolition of

Vivisection, 16a Crane Grove, Islington, London N7 8LB; price £2.95). They also have a very helpful list of charities who fund animal research, others who are doing no research at the moment but may undertake it in the future, and those who do not and will not use animals in this way.

50

SIGN ME UP!

The combined force of a few thousand sparks makes a powerful bolt of lightning.

ARLOW GUTHRIE

It takes only one person to change your life – you.

RUTH CASEY

WHAT NOW?

Now that you have a basic grasp of the things you as an individual can do to help save animals, how about linking up with others who share your passion for compassion? What follows is a list of various organisations, some general in approach, others more specialised, all of which would appreciate your support. By no means is it meant to be comprehensive – such a list would need a whole book of its own – so if you feel you still haven't found the organisation whose goals and tactics are tailor-made for you, keep looking. You will.

General Animal Rights

● Animal Aid: 7 Castle Street, Tonbridge, Kent TN9 1BH; tel. (0732) 364546. Aims to increase public awareness of the abuse of animals in our society while at the same time using peaceful, non-violent forms of protest. Its 'Living Without

Cruelty' campaign, launched in 1985, shows how it is possible to live well without causing suffering to animals. Publishes *Outrage*. *See also* Youth Groups for Animals.

- Animaline: P.O. Box 10, Ryde, Isle of Wight PO33 1JX; tel. (0983) 616980. Conceived by scriptwriter Carla Lane, who is joined by Rita Tushingham and Linda McCartney. Aims to use the media not only to highlight various animal issues, but to stimulate action. Recently involved with the rescue and re-homing of chimpanzees used by Spanish photographers. Also linked with Hartlands Sanctuary, Dorset, where some thirty ponies recently rescued by Animaline arc now living out their lives in safety.

- Animal Protection Foundation: P.O. Box 168, Cardiff CF5 5YH; tel. (0222) 569914. Involved with many and varied animal cruelty issues over past years, the foundation fights for reform in a number of ways – by lecturing, circulating leaflets and petitions, encouraging boycotts. Also organises well-attended and very effective demos. In recent years these have highlighted arctic fox fur farming and poultry battery cages.

- Animus: 34 Marshall Street, London W1V 1LL. Produces a range of seventy-two badges covering every aspect of animal rights. Write to them about having some run off with your own favourite slogan (choice of colours). Ideal way to boost funds for your own particular animal rights group.

- Environmental Investigation Agency (EIA): 208/209 Upper Street, London N1 1RL; tel. (071) 704 9441. Dubbed the 'Eco Detectives' of the environmental world by the Press. Representatives – often working undercover – travel all over the world to carry out in-depth investigations into various issues such as the Faroese Pilot whale hunt, the plight of the African elephant, and the trade in live wildlife. Film footage shot by the EIA frequently used on TV.

- Friends of the Earth (FOE): 26–28 Underwood Street, London N1 7JQ; tel. (071) 490 1555. Works via public education, lobbying of politicians and decision-makers, and collecting information. Has a nationwide network of more than 270 local groups. Publishes *FOE Supporters Newspaper*. *See also* Youth Groups for Animals.

- Friends of the Earth (Scotland) 70–72 New Haven Road, Edinburgh EH6 5QG tel. (031) 554 9977. Separate from the main office, but works in much the same way, co-ordinating supporters' efforts north of the border.
- Greenpeace: Greenpeace House, Canonbury Villas, London N1 2PN; tel. (071) 354 5100/359 7396. An international, independent environmental pressure group which, through direct but non-violent action, tackles the threat to wildlife from direct killing, pollution and habitat loss. One of their most recent campaigns involved the boycott of Icelandic fish to pressure Icelanders to stop slaughtering whales. Publishes a newsletter.
- Royal Society for the Prevention of Cruelty to Animals (RSPCA): The Causeway, Horsham, West Sussex RH12 1HG; tel. (0403) 64181. The world's oldest welfare charity (founded 1840). Works to prevent cruelty not just to cats and dogs, but to all animals, including wildlife and farm animals, those in captivity (such as in circuses), and those who are hunted. Particularly involved at the moment with trying to improve conditions for live animals who are exported (and to prevent the exportation of horses starting again). Also continues to campaign for the instigation of a dog registration scheme (which, the society believes, would ultimately reduce the number of dogs who have to be destroyed each day). Publishes *RSPCA Today*, and *Animal World* for young members.
- Scottish Society for the Prevention of Cruelty to Animals: 19 Melville Street, Edinburgh EH3 7PL; tel. (031) 225 6418. Tackles animal cruelty on all levels, including educational visits to schools. Specific problems include the welfare of a growing population of sheep (some 5,000 were found to be neglected in 1989), sick and orphaned seals along the shoreline, and the re-homing of unwanted cats and dogs (who are neutered free). Dog-fighting is also widespread; the society was recently involved with a court case against an organised dog-fighting ring which resulted in a successful prosecution.

Anti-Vivisection

- Advocates for Animals: 10 Queensferry Street, Edinburgh EH2 4PG; tel. (031) 225 6039. (Formerly the Scottish Society for the Prevention of Vivisection.) The use of animals in experiments is still the principal concern of this society, though it has now widened its scope to include all animal cruelty. In order to achieve its aims, it campaigns for Parliamentary legislation, provides speakers to schools and universities, and holds a wide range of educational material, including videos. Also seeks to make contact with those using animals in an attempt to find common ground. Produces an *Annual Pictorial Review*.
- British Union for the Abolition of Vivisection (BUAV): 16a Crane Grove, Islington, London N7 8LB; tel. (071) 700 4888. Founded in 1898, BUAV is still one of the most active animal rights groups in Britain, concentrating exclusively on the aims for which it was established – the abolition of vivisection. The BUAV logo – a rabbit in a triangle – is appearing on an increasing number of products to show that they are cruelty-free. Publishes *Liberator*.
- National Anti-Vivisection Society (NAVS): 261 Goldhawk Road, London W12 9PE; tel. (081) 846 9777. Working for total prohibition of experiments on living animals and – pending the achievement of this aim – supports partial measures of reform as steps in the right direction. Publishes the *Campaigner*. *See also* Youth Groups for Animals.
- International Association Against Painful Experiments on Animals: P.O. Box 215, St Albans, Hertfordshire AL3 4RD; tel. (0727) 835386. Publishes *International Animal Action*.

Fashion

- Beauty Without Cruelty: 57 King Henry's Walk, London N1 4NH; tel. (071) 254 2929. An educational trust that opposes the commercial slaughter of animals to provide clothing (including fur), fashion accessories and beauty aids. Concentrates its efforts on researching and then publishing facts obtained from around the world. Also promotes the alternatives. Publishes *Compassion*.
- Campaign Against Leather and Fur (CALF): Box 17, 198

Blackstock Road, London N5 1EN. Supplies reasons for avoiding leather and fur, plus advice on tracking down alternatives.

Diet

- Vegan Society (VS): 7 Battle Road, St Leonards-on-Sea, East Sussex TN37 7AA; tel. (0424) 427393. Everything you need to know about becoming vegan from cooking to clothing, where to eat, what to buy, and more besides. Publishes the *Vegan*.
- Vegetarian Society (UK) Ltd.: Parkdale, Dunham Road, Altrincham, Cheshire WA14 4QG; tel. (061) 928 0793. Provides recipes, information on vegetarian foods, arranges Cordon Vert and other cookery courses, plus a wide range of other activities to help promote vegetarianism. Publishes the *Vegetarian*.

Factory Farming

- Compassion in World Farming: 20 Lavant Street, Petersfield, Hampshire GU32 3EW; tel. (0730) 64208/68863. Petitions against cruel export practices, inhumane slaughter and intensive confinement (battery) systems. Publishes *Agscene*. *See also* Youth Groups for Animals.
- Chickens' Lib: P.O. Box 2, Holmfirth, Huddersfield, Yorkshire HD7 1QT; tel. (0484) 688650. Provides leaflets, stickers, posters and videos. A constant challenge to British agriculture's abominable treatment of both chickens and turkeys.

Religion and Animals

- Anglican Society for Animal Welfare: St Augustine's Vicarage, 117 Queen's Gate, London SW7 5LW. Promotes prayer, study and action on behalf of all animals. The Bishop of Salisbury is a patron of the society. Member of the CCCWA.
- Catholic Study Circle for Animal Welfare: 39 Onslow Gardens, South Woodford, London E18 1ND. Organises conferences, visits to animal sanctuaries, pilgrimages. Publishes the *Ark*. Member of the CCCWA.

- Christian Consultative Council for the Welfare of Animals (CCCWA): 269 Belstead Road, Ipswich, Suffolk 1P2 9DY. A collection of Christian animal welfare/rights societies of which fourteen are based in Britain, their aim being to encourage and co-ordinate joint action amongst Christians and those of other religious faiths on behalf of animals. Includes bigger societies, as well as groups such as Christian Ecology Link and the Willow Tree Sanctuary for Animal Welfare. Most recent issues: hunting on church land and factory farming. Organises Retreat Weekends for Animals.
- International Jewish Vegetarian Society: 855 Finchley Road, London NW11 8LX; tel. (081) 455 0692. Founded twenty-seven years ago in order to revive and make known the great vegetarian teachings of the Jewish faith. Publishes the *Jewish Vegetarian* which includes news, views and recipes.
- Pagan Animal Rights: 23 Highfield South, Rock Ferry, Wirral L42 4NA. Starts with the premise that our treatment of the Earth and all beings deeply offends both the Goddess/God within and without, and therefore advocates the treatment of the Earth with respect. Works towards the same aims as other animal rights societies and in many of the same ways, but also includes meditation and ritual magic where appropriate.
- Quaker Concern for Animal Welfare: Webb's Cottage, Woolpits Road, Saling, Braintree, Essex CM7 5DZ. A pressure group that has been in existence for over 100 years. Sees the traditional Quaker Peace Testimony as extending to all creatures, and therefore encourages Friends to try to live without dependence on cruelty. Member of the CCCWA.

Anti Blood Sports

- Campaign for the Abolition of Angling: P.O. Box 130, Sevenoaks, Kent TN14 5NR. Provides information, merchandise, and a newsletter, *Pisces*.
- Dartmoor Badgers Protection League: Riverside Cottage, Poundsgate, Devon TQ13 7NV. One of the original badger protection groups, working hard in an area where there are many badger setts under threat from growing numbers of

baiters. Supporters always appreciated, even if they do not live locally.

- Hunt Saboteurs Association (HSA): P.O. Box 1, Carlton, Nottingham, Nottinghamshire NG4 2JY; tel. (0602) 590357. Actually goes into the field to sabotage the hunt. Though activists are always needed (they have over a thousand 'active' members), your support also counts for a lot. Publishes *Howl*. *See also* 'Fox Cubs' under Youth Groups for Animals.

- League Against Cruel Sports: 83–97 Union Street, London SE1 1SG; tel. (071) 407 0979. Politically active against the hunting of foxes, deer, hares, otters (sometimes urging the adoption of drag-hunting as an alternative). Well-presented information pack gives you all the facts you need to argue your case convincingly. Publishes *Cruel Sports*.

- National Federation of Badger Groups: 16 Ashdown Gardens, Sanderstead, South Croydon, Surrey CR2 9DR; tel. (081) 657 4636. Will put you in touch with your nearest local group who will welcome any support in patrolling setts.

Direct Action

- Animal Liberation Front Supporters Group (ALF): BCM Box 1160, London WC1N 3XX. Since its formation in 1976, ALF activists have saved many thousands of animals from death and suffering. In return for their compassion, some 150 of them have been imprisoned, and many more have been fined. The ALF Supporters Group (which now incorporates Support Animal Rights Prisoners) exists to provide the activists with encouragement and funds.

Fur

- Lynx: P.O. Box 300, Nottingham, Nottinghamshire NG1 5HN; tel. (0602) 413052. Frontline anti-fur campaigners, highlighting both fur factory farms and the killing of wild animals. Shops in London's Covent Garden and Cambridge (more planned), and ads everywhere.

Marine Mammals

- Dolphin Circle: 8 Dolby Road, London SW6 3NE. Covers all

aspects of dolphin welfare, including getting them out of dolphinaria, and trying to help clean up their natural environment, the sea. Publishes a quarterly magazine.

- International Dolphin Watch: Parklands, North Ferriby, Humberside HU14 3ET; tel. (0482) 643403. Founded by Horace Dobbs, who has written a number of books on dolphins and made countless radio, television and personal appearances. His work on the positive effect contact with dolphins may have on human beings (a project he calls 'Operation Sunflower') gives hope that results will provide yet another reason for halting the slaughter of these gentle creatures.

- Sea Shepherd UK: P.O. Box 5, Ashford, Middlesex TW15 2PY; tel. (0784) 254846. The British branch of the American marine conservation society that is well known for its direct action on the seas. Its latest campaign is to raise Japanese awareness of the damage they are causing to the planet, and to pressure or persuade them to stop this. UK supporters much needed.

- Whale and Dolphin Conservation Society: 19a James Street West, Bath, Avon BA1 2BT; tel. (0225) 334511. Working to help whales and dolphins in their own environment, and also those in captivity. Involved recently in the bid to persuade the British tuna industry to adopt a strict code of practice regarding the use of drift nets to reduce the massive incidental destruction of dolphins. Has international links. Publishes *Sonar*.

Circuses and Zoos

- Captive Animals' Protection Society: 36 Braemore Court, Kingsway, Hove, East Sussex BN3 4FG; tel. (0273) 737756. Concentrates on the plight of animals in circuses in Britain and overseas, though concerned also for animals kept in zoos, wildlife parks and dolphinaria.

- Zoo Check: Cherry Tree Cottage, Coldharbour, Dorking, Surrey RH5 6HA; tel. (0306) 712091. Public watchdog organisation seeking zoo reforms as well as helping to conserve wildlife in its natural habitat. Includes Elefriends (campaigning specifically to stop elephants being slaughtered

for their ivory) and Junior Elefriends (*see* Youth Groups for
Animals).

Animal Rescue/Emergency

- Blue Cross: Shilton Road, Burford, Oxford OX8 4PF; tel.
  (0993) 822651. Has sixteen branches and three hospitals.
  Medical care and re-homing – mainly cats and dogs, though
  other animals (including horses and donkeys) also taken in if
  necessary. Free how-to-care-for booklets provided to
  anyone taking an animal. Publishes the *Blue Cross Illustrated*,
  and *Pawprints* for young supporters.
- National Animal Rescue Association: 21 Highlands Avenue,
  Spinney Hill, Northampton NN3 1BG; tel. (0604) 647552.
  Accident and emergency service that works nationwide to
  help with anything from minor problems such as a cat up a
  tree, to major disasters like the Humber Estuary spill. No
  animal outside their scope. Twenty-four-hour phone number
  (but please use out of office hours in case of extreme
  emergency only).
- People's Dispensary for Sick Animals (PDSA): Whitechapel
  Way, Priorslee, Telford, Shropshire TF2 9PQ; tel. (0952)
  290999. Has fifty-seven treatment centres and provides aid in
  seventy communities (linked with local vets) in order to offer
  free medical attention for the companion animals of those
  who cannot afford to pay. Vital to funds are the many PDSA
  shops which always need volunteer helpers.
- Swan Song (formerly Swan Rescue Service): P.O. Box 3,
  Beccles, Suffolk NR34 0DF. Fighting against indifference
  and on the smallest of budgets to help the big white birds.
  Particularly concerned about the many deaths caused by
  casual fishermen and overhead electricity cables.
- Wildlife Hospital Trust: 1 Pembleton Close, Aylesbury,
  Buckinghamshire HP21 7NY; tel. (0296) 29860. Nurses more
  than 4,000 injured birds and animals every year. In 1990
  established Europe's first wildlife teaching hospital. Particularly concerned about hedgehogs, for whom it has a special
  treatment centre – St Tiggywinkles.

Cats and Dogs

- Cats Protection League: 17 King's Road, Horsham, West Sussex RH13 5PP; tel. (0403) 65566. Objectives are to rescue strays and re-home them when possible, and to encourage neutering. Has eleven shelters providing temporary accommodation, some also having facilities for long-term residents, and others taking boarders to help fund the league's work.

- National Canine Defence League: 1 Pratt Mews, London NW1 0AD; tel. (071) 388 0137. Britain's largest canine rescue charity with a policy that no healthy dog in their care is ever destroyed. Rescue centres across the country. Campaigns locally and nationally on all dog-related subjects.

- National Petwatch: P.O. Box 16, Brighouse, West Yorkshire HD6 1DS; tel. (0484) 722411. Formed in response to the belief that companion animals are being systematically stolen throughout the country, usually for laboratories or the fur trade. Collates data as evidence with which to alert the public. Works with the police.

- Puppy Watch: P.O. Box 23, Neath, West Glamorgan, Wales SA11 1QP; tel. (0639) 845755. A small but vociferous group of people concerned about the breeding of pedigree dogs on the notorious 'puppy farms' that are dotted around the country, but especially prolific in West Wales. Getting a lot of valuable publicity. You don't have to live there to be a supporter!

British Wildlife

- British Hedgehog Preservation Society: Knowbury House, Knowbury, Ludlow, Shropshire SY8 3LQ. Provides leaflets on every aspect of hedgehogs, including hibernation, dangers (such as cattle-grids) and what to do about them, how to care for orphaned hoglets. Educates and funds research to work for the survival of hedgehogs in Britain.

- Horses and Ponies Protection Association: 64 Station Road, Padiham, Near Burnley, Lancashire BB12 8EF; tel. (0282) 79138.

- London Wildlife Trust: Central Office, 80 York Way, London N1 9AG; tel. (071) 278 6612. Makes London a better place to live – and not just for humans. Has some sixty sites, and provides leaflets on many of the animals who can be found there (including kestrels). 'Watch' is the children's branch of the trust, formed so that children can have fun as well as learn about wildlife. Adult members receive newsletter, annual review, and *Natural World* (published by the RSNC).

- Royal Society for Nature Conservation (RSNC): The Green, Nettleham, Lincoln LN2 2NR; tel. (0522) 752326. Has associated local trusts to help wildlife around the country, some managing sites – many of which are in urban environments. Contact them for details. Also publishes *Natural World*. See also Youth Group for Animals.
- Royal Society for the Protection of Birds (RSPB): The Lodge, Sandy, Bedfordshire SG19 2DL: tel. (0767) 680551. Works to conserve wild birds in numerous ways including lobbying Parliament, supplying printed information and videos, and organising film shows and talks. Has nature reserves around the country.

Non-Animal Research

- Dr Hadwen Trust for Humane Research: 6c Brand Street, Hitchin, Hertfordshire SG5 1RD; tel. (0462) 436819. Established in 1970 to promote the development of humane alternatives to animal experiments. Funds promising research projects not involving animals. Interesting range of posters and other display material, also a selection of items including Honesty skin care and household products.
- Humane Research Trust: Brook House, 29 Bramhall Lane South, Bramhall, Cheshire SK7 2DN; tel. (061) 439 8041. Established to help scientists who are working on cures for diseases to find new methods other than the use of animals. Awards grants to specific projects, the most recent being research into cataracts. Organises talks for both the scientific community and the general public.
- Lord Dowding Fund: 261 Goldhawk Road, London W12 9PE; tel. (081) 846 9777. Linked to NAVS. Funds scientists who are using humane alternatives to animal research.

Educational

- Athene Trust: 3a Charles Street, Petersfield, Hampshire GU32 3EH; tel. (0730) 68070. Works with schools to promote the essential harmony which could and should exist between all mankind and the natural world. Sees this happening through a regeneration of organic/veganic farming, conservation of wildlife, and improvements to the welfare of animals on farms.

- Animals' Vigilantes: James Mason House, 24 Salisbury Street, Fordingbridge, Hampshire SP6 1AF; tel. (0425) 653663. An educational trust pledged to fight all cruelty to animals. Accepts that this work can be successful only if future generations recognise man's responsibility towards animal life, so concentrates on instilling a reverence for all life in young people. Believes in the value of working with other societies when necessary to help relieve specific cases of animal suffering.

Politics

- Green Party Animal Rights Working Group: 23 Highfield South, Rock Ferry, Wirral L42 4NA. Welcomes all members of the Green Party who have suggestions or questions about the party's policies regarding animals. Provides contact point for non-members who are interested in knowing more.

Groups for Animals

- Disabled Against Animal Research and Exploitation: P.O. Box 8, Daventry, Northamptonshire NN11 4RQ. Welcomes support of those disabled who wish to support their campaign to help relieve the suffering of animals.

- Doctors in Britain Against Animal Experiments (DBAE): P.O. Box 302, London N8 9HD. Formed in 1990 by a group of doctors, concerned about the use of animals in experiments and resolved to try and reduce it.

- GEMMA (Gay Vegetarians and Vegans): BCM Box 5700, London WC1N 3XX. An informal group formed in 1979 to provide a friendship network and encouragement for gay people who are – or are considering becoming – vegetarian. Regular meetings in London, contacts in other areas. Puts out a newsletter (print and tape).

- Nurses Anti-Vivisection Movement: Hillcrest Cottage, 2 Hillcrest, Uppertown, Bonsall, Derbyshire DE4 2AW; tel. (062982) 4664. Brings together nurses, in their professional capacity, to publicly denounce experiments on animals, especially those conducted during the testing of drugs and in the field of behavioural sciences.
- Teachers for Animal Rights: 29 Lynwood Road, London SW17 8SB. Run by a full-time primary school teacher. Exists in order to disseminate information about animal rights issues to both schools and teachers, particularly those linked to the educational system (such as dissection and school meals). Sends out information sheet plus leaflets.
- Writers Against Experiments on Animals: Wessington Court, Woolhope, Hereford HR1 4QN; tel. (0432) 860603. A group formed in the belief that the power of the pen should be used by professionals on behalf of animals. Invites the support of all writers to pressure people and Parliament to acknowledge the inalienable right of all living creatures to be free from exploitation.

Youth Groups for Animals

- Animals' Defenders: 261 Goldhawk Road, London W12 9PE; tel. (081) 846 9777. The junior branch of NAVS. For any youngsters aged eight to eighteen who want to make the planet a better place for animals. Publishes a quarterly magazine *Animals' Defenders*.
- Animal Aid Youth Group: 7 Castle Street, Tonbridge, Kent TN9 1BH; tel. (0732) 364546. Very active, with a regular newsletter telling members what other members are doing in their areas to help spread the message that animals have rights. Includes such issues as dissection in schools, and how abusing animals also endangers the planet.
- Earth Action: 26-28 Underwood Street, London N1 7JQ; tel. (071) 490 1555. The youth section of FOE. Encourages concern about the environment, and shows ways to put this concern into action.
- Farm Animal Rangers: 20 Lavant Street, Petersfield, Hampshire GU32 3EW; tel. (0730) 64208. Associated with Compassion in World Farming. Tells youngsters the truth

about factory farming and asks them to help in the campaign to stop such animal abuses.

- Fox Cubs: P.O. Box 1, Carlton, Nottingham NG4 2JY; tel. (0602) 590357. The youth section of the Hunt Saboteurs Association.
- Junior Elefriends: Cherry Tree Cottage, Coldharbour, Dorking, Surrey RH5 6HA; tel. (0306) 712091. Teaches young people why elephants are worth saving, and then shows them ways to help the Elefriend campaign to stop the wholesale slaughter of elephants for their ivory.
- SCREAM (School Campaign for Reaction Against Meat): Parkdale, Dunham Road, Altrincham, Cheshire WA14 4QG; tel. (061) 928 0793. The youth group of the Vegetarian Society. Provides support for young vegetarians and vegans at school, and suggestions for encouraging fellow students to join them.
- Watch: The Green, Nettleham, Lincoln LN2 2NR; tel. (0522) 752326. Junior wing of the RSNV. Encourages youngsters to take part on both a local and national level.

International/Overseas

- Anglo-Italian Society for the Protection of Animals: 136 Baker Street, London W1M 1FH. A British organisation that helps fund various sanctuaries in Italy, particularly those created to either house or re-home the very many stray cats and dogs.
- Brooke Hospital for Animals: 1/3 Regent Street, London SW1Y 4PA; tel. (071) 930 0210. Started in Cairo in the 1930s – initially to rescue the old English cavalry horses who had been sold at the end of the First World War, then to offer medical help to the working animals of the poor – and still going strong. Now also has clinics in Luxor, Aswan and Petra in Jordan, plus plans to open one in India. Apart from helping sick animals and teaching local people how to keep them healthy, has a policy of buying animals who are beyond help and giving them a week of luxury in the kraals before humanely destroying them.
- Care for the Wild: 1 Ashfolds, Horsham Road, Rusper, Horsham, West Sussex RH12 4QX; tel. (0293) 871596.

Involved with combating cruelty and exploitation and alleviating suffering in all species of wildlife both in the UK and abroad. Injects money directly into specific projects (such as the Elephant Orphanage in Kenya). Works with a dedicated network of field workers and investigators to provide the media and public with accurate information, so motivating everyone to take action before it is too late.

- Greek Animal Rescue: 30 Macdonald Road, Friern Barnet, London N11 3JB; tel. (081) 361 2430. Helps fund the work of shelters run by local people who are endeavouring to feed and find homes for at least some of the pitiful strays who are everywhere on the Greek mainland and islands. Also stresses the important role tourists play in helping animals, especially – for example – by boycotting the use of the donkeys, most of whom lead such miserable and hard lives.

- Green Flag International Ltd: P.O. Box 396, Linton, Cambridge CB1 6UL. Aims to make tourism environmentally friendly! A newly formed UK company working in partnership with tour operators and travel organisations to make improvements to the environment worldwide, which in turn helps wildlife.

- International Council for Bird Preservation: 32 Cambridge Road, Girton, Cambridge CB3 0PJ; tel. (0223) 277318. Devoted entirely to the conservation of birds and their habitats, with projects taking place throughout the world. Within the organisation are specialised clubs such as the World Bird Club and the Rare Bird Club. Publishes a newsletter called *World Bird Watch*.

- International League for the Protection of Horses: Overa House Farm, Larling, Norwich, Norfolk NR16 2QX; tel. (0953) 717309. Founded in 1927 for the protection of horses being sent to abattoirs on the Continent. Has three Rest and Rehabilitation Centres in Britain looking after some 630 rescued equines. Offices and representatives are also to be found in countries where mistreatment of horses is rife, including Morocco, Greece and Israel. Has a junior club, and publishes a high-quality quarterly newsletter.

- International Primate Protection League: 116 Judd Street,

London WC1H 9NS; tel. (071) 837 7227. Concerned with the welfare and conservation of all primates, including their abuse and mistreatment, and the destruction of the environment in which they live. Endeavours to place rescued primates in new homes such as wildlife parks.

- Society for the Protection of Animals in North Africa (SPANA): 15 Buckingham Gate, London SW1E 6LB; tel. (071) 828 0997. Actively engaged in education about and the protection of all animals in North Africa, with refuges and clinics to which sick or homeless animals can be taken.
- World Society for the Protection of Animals (WSPA): Park Place, 10 Lawn Lane, London SW8 1UD; tel. (071) 793 0540. Concerned about many issues, including emergency relief worldwide in case of flood or earthquake, the slaughter of migratory birds, animal sacrifices in Cuba, Publishes *Animals International*.

For a more extensive list:
- Rainbow Database, Rainbow Centre, 180 Mansfield Road, Nottingham NG1 3HU.